# Murder in East Anglia

## ROBERT CHURCH

## ROBERT HALE · LONDON

*By the same author*
Accidents of Murder
More Murder in East Anglia

To
Dorothy

ISBN 0 7090 5205 7

Robert Hale Limited
Clerkenwell House
Clerkenwell Green
London EC1R 0HT

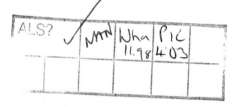

Printed and bound by
Interprint, Valletta, Malta

# Contents

# Scenes of the Crimes

*Mary Jane Bennett* South beach, rear of Botton's Pleasure Beach Amusements. O/S Sheet no 134. British National Grid Reference TG 532062. Row 104, South Quay, approximately ¼ mile south of Town Hall. O/S no 134 British National Grid Reference TG 523072

*Archibald Brown* Rayleigh church (Holy Trinity), Hockley Road. O/S Sheet no 178; BNG Ref TQ 809909

*Alexander Wollaston and Francis Willis* King's College, Cambridge. O/S Sheet no 154; BNG Ref TL 447583

*Rose Harsent* Peasenhall Village. A1120. Gardiner's house; Providence House; Doctor's Chapel, all still in existence. O/S Sheet 156; BNG Ref TM 355693

*Leonard Thomas Gilford* Hockering Wood, ½ mile north of Hockering Village on A47. O/S Sheet no 133; BNG Ref TG 073145

*Camille Cecile Holland* Moat Farm (Coldham's Farm), approximately 1½ miles east of Clavering village. O/S Sheet no 167: BNG Ref TL 494320

*Cacilie Wollner* Emery Street, Petersfield, off Mill Road, Cambridge. O/S Sheet no 154; BNG Ref TL 461581.

*Winifred Mary Evans* Lane on right-hand side of Ellough Road, (B1127), approximately 1¼ miles from the junction with Lowestoft Road. O/S Sheet no 156; BNG Ref TM 442885.

*Isaac Jermy and Son* Stanfield Hall, 2 miles due east of Wymondham. O/S Sheet no 144; BNG Ref TG 144010

*William Sweet* Byron's Pool off Grantchester to Trumpington Road. O/S Sheet no 154; BNG Ref TL 435545

*George Gutteridge* Stapleford Road (B175), approximately ½ mile north of Stapleford Abbotts. O/S Sheet no 177; BNG Ref TQ 502954.

# Acknowledgements

I wish to thank the following for helping in various ways with this book. The order in which the names are given does not necessarily indicate the amount of assistance given.

Mr B.R. Cole of Framingham Earl, an acknowledged expert on many East Anglian crimes, who gave unstintingly of his time and hospitality; Detective Inspector Alan Hill of the Essex Police, who helped me far beyond the call of his normal duty; David Wright and Rosemary Rogers, librarians, and their ever helpful staff at the Local Records Department, Lowestoft Central Library; the County Archivists and the staffs of the Norfolk, Suffolk, Essex and Cambridgeshire Record Offices; the librarians and members of staff at the Cambridge Central, Romford and Southend libraries; Alan Atherton and the staff of the *Eastern Daily Press* library at Norwich; Barbara Green and the staff of Norwich Castle Museum Archaeological Department; the staff of the *Southend Standard Recorder* library; Linda Devine, Beccles; Sue Copeland, Brentwood; the Metropolitan Police Records Office staff; various individuals manning the Home Office (Prison) press desk.

George G. Harrap Ltd., London; Butterworth & Co., Sevenoaks; William Hodge & Co Ltd., Glasgow, for permission to quote from published works.

Finally, the anonymous reporters of *The Times, Daily Mirror, Eastern Daily Press, Cambridge News,* the *Southend Standard* and the *Essex Times,* whose accounts of several cases have supplemented other research.

King's Lynn

Leonard GILFORD
HOCKERING WOOD

Norwich

Isaac JERMY Snr
Isaac JERMY Jnr
WYMONDHAM

Mary BENNETT
GREAT YARMOUTH

Lowestoft

Peterborough

Winifred EVANS
ELLOUGH

Thetford

Huntingdon

Rose HARSENT
PEASENHALL

Alexander WOLLASTON &
Francis WILLIS        Cacilie WOLLNER
CAMBRIDGE          CAMBRIDGE

Bury St
Edmunds

William SWEET
BYRON'S POOL

Ipswich

Camille HOLLAND
CLAVERING

Sudbury

Bishop's
Stortford

Colchester

Miles
0                    20

George GUTTERIDGE
HOWE GREEN

0                    20
km

Chelmsford

Archibald BROWN
RAYLEIGH

LONDON

Southend-on-Sea

*Murder in East Anglia*

# Introduction

Millions of words have been written extolling the undoubted appeal and charm of East Anglia.

However, like other areas of the British Isles, there is a darker side to the region. During the past 150 years numerous murders have been committed within its boundaries, some well known, others less familiar, while the majority attracted little attention at the time and were soon forgotten.

Many of these crimes have been well documented, others less so; in this book I have drawn upon a variety of sources in an attempt to describe and reconstruct a selection of cases that I hope the reader will find of interest.

Space has not permitted a detailed account or analysis, so I apologize for any obvious omissions. Similarly, I accept responsibility for theories advanced and conclusions drawn, with either of which the reader may agree or not, but which I hope will at least provoke further thought.

R.C.

# 1  Death on the Dunes, Norfolk 1900

An assortment of Victorian murderers attained a degree of notoriety that ensured their names passed into criminal folklore. George Joseph Smith, the 'Brides in the Bath' killer; the mass poisoners William Palmer and Doctor Neill Cream; Charlie Peace, the burglar hanged for killing a neighbour's wife, and probably the best known of all, Jack the Ripper, the undetected slayer of London's East End prostitutes, are but a few of those whose names have become synonymous with nineteenth-century murders.

Surprisingly, in view of the nationwide interest it attracted, the case of Herbert John Bennett, accused of murdering his wife in what became known as 'The Yarmouth Beach Murder', did not attain such renown. As the *Eastern Daily Press* later pointed out, the case provided 'a blend of mystery, romance, tragedy and pathos'. Certainly it contained the real-life ingredients of the melodramas so enjoyed by Victorian theatregoers. A young, golden-haired victim; her husband, tall and strong, with dark hair and a waxed moustache, accused of strangling her, and the innocent young parlour maid who had surrendered her heart to the accused man.

Five months earlier the summer season had been drawing to a close at Great Yarmouth. Racegoers had flocked to the flat racing season's final meeting on 18 and 19 September, while in the evening many others converged on the Theatre Royal where the musical comedy *Skipped by the Light of the Moon* was the attraction.

The early morning of Sunday, 23 September saw John Norton, a fifteen-year-old local boy, on the way to his job as a bathing hut attendant on Yarmouth's south beach. Crossing the sandhills he noticed a young woman apparently asleep. Closer scrutiny, and sight of a bootlace tightly knotted around her throat, convinced him that he was looking at a dead rather than a slumbering woman, so without further ado he raced away to report his find.

Any detective will confirm that the first, vital step to be taken in a murder investigation is to identify the victim. The mode of death may be obvious, but the motive will often remain obscure until the identity is established. In the case of the young woman found on Great Yarmouth beach, that task was to prove more difficult than anticipated.

When found she had been dressed fashionably and expensively. Despite this, the woman with the light-coloured, curly hair carried nothing by which she could immediately be identified. Nonetheless all seemed to go well; later on the Sunday morning Mrs Eliza Rudrum, a Yarmouth landlady, went to the police station and reported that a young woman lodger called Hood had gone out the previous evening and failed to return. Mrs Rudrum said that the woman had arrived with her baby, seeking accommodation on the evening of Saturday, 15 September, saying that she had come from Yorkshire with her brother-in-law, who was in love with her and was staying elsewhere in the town. During the ensuing week the visitor had regularly come and gone from her lodgings, and on two or three occasions had been seen out in men's company. An expected letter had arrived late on Friday, 21 September. Postmarked 'Woolwich' and addressed to Mrs Hood, part of it she read out to her landlady 'Meet me at the big clock at nine o'clock, and put your babe to bed'. Unfortunately the letter disappeared and was never found.

The next day the lodger had spent indoors until the evening when she had gone out for the last time. As she left her landlady casually noticed that she was still wearing around her neck the silver watch on a gold chain that she had habitually worn during her stay. Her departure that evening was not the last to be seen of Mrs Hood by one of the Rudrums. Daughter Alice saw her at about nine o'clock standing outside Yarmouth town hall, a building featuring a 'big clock'. After exchanging a few words, Alice continued on her way, never to see the other woman again.

After listening to Mrs Rudrum, Detective Inspector Robert Lingwood who, together with William Parker, Yarmouth's Chief Constable, had taken charge of the investigation, acted swiftly. Accompanying the landlady home, he searched the room that had lately been occupied by her lodger. There he found a beach snapshot showing her with a young child, and a purse containing the return half of a first-class rail ticket dated 15 September, from

Great Yarmouth to Liverpool Street.

The Yarmouth officers made every effort to have the dead woman identified. Her photograph was circulated to police forces throughout the land and enquiries were made by the Metropolitan Police at Woolwich to try and trace the author of the mysterious letter, while yet more enquiries were made at hotels in Great Yarmouth in the hope of tracing her brother-in-law. Her costume manufacturer in London was seen and asked if he could provide a clue to her identity. All in vain – the dead woman defied all efforts to identify her. In the meantime a post-mortem revealed that death had been from asphyxia as the result of strangulation.

An inquest scheduled to open on 25 September, was twice adjourned until the 27th. At the end of two days, with the dead woman still unidentified, there was a third adjournment until 29 October. On 28 September, with the inquest in progress, a quiet ceremony took place unnoticed in the parish churchyard of St Nicholas. In a plain redwood coffin, with two small decorative shields on the lid, the dead woman was interred. The few mourners included Mrs Rudrum, her daughter and Detective Inspector Lingwood. The Parish Register described the coffin's occupant as 'The Unknown', with the name 'Hood' in parenthesis.

On 30 October, thirty-eight days after the body had been found, the Coroner's jury returned a verdict of 'Wilful murder against some person unknown by a man unknown'.

Whilst police enquiries continued throughout October and early November, but with no arrest, press and public interest in the case predictably waned, the national papers devoting their space to other news.

In South Africa the Boer War had just entered its second year, while at home a general election saw a former war correspondent named Winston Churchill begin what was destined to be a long and distinguished parliamentary career when he was elected as Member of Parliament for Oldham.

Back in Great Yarmouth two young golf caddies of eleven and twelve years took time off from their caddying to place two chairs on the railway line adjoining the golf course. A passing train struck the obstacles, fortunately without serious consequences. The boys were not so lucky, each receiving six strokes of the birch.

Public interest in the Bennett case was suddenly reawakened on 7 November, by headline news that on the previous evening at Woolwich a man had been arrested by Metropolitan Police officers and charged with the murder of the woman found six weeks earlier on Great Yarmouth beach.

The arrest of twenty-one-year-old Herbert John Bennett had been carried out quietly and unobtrusively in Beresford Street, Woolwich, by Detective Chief Inspector Alfred Leach and Sergeant Oldfield of New Scotland Yard, as the suspect left the Arsenal, where he worked as a labourer. Bennett accompanied the officers to Woolwich police station where they met up with Chief Constable Parker, and where later they were joined by Detective Inspector Lingwood. When charged Bennett adopted the line he was to maintain throughout by replying, 'I don't know what you mean, I have never been to Yarmouth.'

After the charging the Chief Constable and a Detective Inspector went to Bennett's room at 18, William Street, where in a suitcase they found a silver watch and gold chain, two items that were later to figure prominently at the trial.

The following day at Bennett's request, a young woman named Alice Meadows called at the police station where they were allowed a few minutes together.

On the Saturday morning, after his return to Great Yarmouth the previous evening, Bennett, neatly dressed in a black, three-quarter length coat and wearing a hard felt hat, made his first appearance in Yarmouth police court. Standing composed and attentive in the dock he replied, 'not guilty' to the murder indictment. He listened impassively as evidence of identification of the deceased woman, and of his arrest, was given by Yarmouth's Chief Constable. At the end of the hearing he was remanded to Norwich prison until 16 November 1900.

During his week on remand Bennett received a poignant letter from Alice Meadows in which she told him, 'not to think of me if that was your wife. Think of your child. Pray to God, and if you have committed this crime ask for forgiveness. I will pray for you.'

The Quarter Sessions court at Great Yarmouth was overflowing with spectators when the committal proceedings opened on 16 November. The case had attracted so much national interest that the hearing had been transferred from the police court to the larger Quarter Sessions in order to accommodate the considerable number of reporters and members of the public expected to attend. So it proved: when Bennett stepped into the dock that Friday morning, reporters had spilled from the jury box onto the civic benches, while in the public gallery a crowd mainly of women craned forward, anxious to catch a glimpse of him.

Bennett evinced no surprise at the number of people present as he glanced around the court. Dressed in the familiar three-quarter length overcoat, tightly buttoned but with a white collar and blue tie showing above, he merely smiled slightly in recognition at his parents who had travelled up from Kent and had been found seats immediately behind the dock.

The preliminary hearing, which was to last four days, could be likened to the supporting bout on the night of a championship fight. The relatively lightweight solicitors, Mr G.J. Wiltshire for the Treasury and Mr E. Ely Robb, a prominent Tunbridge Wells lawyer representing Bennett, battling it out at the lower court, before the heavyweight counsel, in the persons of Mr Charles Gill, KC and Mr Edward Marshall Hall KC, faced each other at the Old Bailey.

The story which unfolded at the police court and later at the Old Bailey (or Central Criminal Court as it should properly be called), had begun four years earlier when in 1896 Mary Jane Clarke, a nineteen-year-old butcher's daughter living at Northfleet in Kent, and already an accomplished musician, took on sixteen-year-old Herbert John Bennett as her music pupil. The couple had soon fallen in love and had married in July the following year. Almost immediately they had embarked on a life of deception and petty crime.

Who first conceived the idea of buying up a large quantity of cheap violins and then reselling them at over five times their purchase price is not known, but the enterprise was to prove highly lucrative. To sell the instruments, Mrs Bennett cast herself in the roles of a bereaved widow forced to sell her late husband's violin to obtain money to buy food, an impecunious medical student and even as the deprived wife of a clergyman. By these methods the couple had soon amassed £1,200, a small fortune in the late nineteenth century.

Bennett, not to be outshone by his enterprising young wife, set himself up as a jewellery and sewing machine salesman; months later there were still wholesalers in the Midlands seeking to retrieve their jewellery samples! Notwithstanding such minor peccadillos, their joint efforts enabled the Bennetts to move out of their Balham lodgings at the beginning of 1900 and buy themselves a grocery shop at Westgate-on-Sea, into which they moved with their two-year-old daughter Ruby. Fortunately the family were out when a few weeks later the premises mysteriously caught fire and were gutted. They collected the insurance money, and undaunted promptly bought another shop which they stocked up on credit, giving little thought to paying their suppliers.

By March 1900 the Bennetts had been living on their wits for over two-and-a-half years. Now with the baying of creditors and disgruntled violin customers sounding ever louder, the couple departed for South Africa, leaving Ruby with Bennett's grandfather at Gravesend. The reason for this sudden journey was never discovered, although Marshall Hall later voiced his belief that Bennett had decided to try his hand at spying for the Boers. Wherever the truth lay, the couple returned to England a mere two months later. On 12 May 1900, Mrs Bennett called at an address at Plumstead, South London, coincidentally the home of a police constable and his wife, and for ten shillings a week rented in the name of Bartlett two rooms for herself, her husband and baby. After explaining to the landlady that her husband was due back from South Africa the same evening she immediately left for Great Yarmouth to collect Ruby, who for some unexplained reason was now at the resort. She was thus not at home to greet her husband, an omission that was to lead to a blazing row between them when she returned two days later.

Although Mrs Bennett tried her best to appear a loving and devoted wife, it soon became apparent that all was not well between the couple. Rows were frequent, Bennett being particularly abusive, frequently ordering his wife to 'shut your great mouth'. She didn't lack spirit, rounding on him one day when he threatened to leave her and Ruby to tell him, 'Herbert, I will follow you for the sake of the baby, and if you are not careful I can get you fifteen years', an apparent reference to her husband's former misdemeanours. He replied menacingly, 'I wish you were dead, and if you are not careful you soon will be.' On another occasion when he was late home, his wife was heard to remark, 'I suppose you have been after the other beauty again.'

With such acrimony, and there being little doubt that Bennett was philandering, the domestic situation could not endure. With Mrs Bennett's suspicions and accusations of infidelity, matters came to a head a month after their return from South Africa when on 15 June Bennett walked out on his wife and daughter and took rooms in Union Street, Woolwich, passing himself off as a single man.

Mrs Bennett, alias Bartlett, moved into lodgings with Ruby at Bexleyheath in Kent, where her husband continued to visit them occasionally throughout July and August whilst he was working at the Woolwich Arsenal. These visits did nothing to restore harmony between the couple. On the contrary, on the eve of his wife's move in early July 1900, to a small rented house nearby, Bennett called and was overheard telling her that he ... 'would never live with you again, or sleep in the same room with you'.

It may have been coincidental, but on or very near the date Bennett made that remark, a new love entered his life, one who was to innocently precipitate the tragic events that were to follow.

Alice Meadows was a young parlour maid working in London's West End when she was introduced to Bennett by the cook, who was already acquainted with him. Bennett was immediately attracted to the demure young servant girl, while she in turn was flattered by the amorous and constant attention he paid her. When asked about him later Alice was reported to have said ... 'he is a very attractive man, and he seemed very fond of me'. So fond of her indeed that Bennett persuaded her to spend the August bank holiday with him at Great Yarmouth, where they occupied separate rooms at the Crown and Anchor hotel. At the end of the month they journeyed further afield, to Ireland for two weeks holiday. On the morning of their departure, Bennett proposed to Alice, was accepted and gave her an engagement ring; they agreed to get married the following June.

Up until now Bennett's dallying had remained almost entirely unhindered by the fact that he had a wife and young daughter living not far away. Now, with his betrothal to Alice they presented a more urgent problem, one that was to inspire that which was to follow.

We arrive now at the final week in the life of Mary Jane Bennett and the sequence of events that were to culminate in her death.

On Saturday 15 September, after telling neighbours that she was going with her husband and Ruby for a holiday to Yorkshire, she left instead with the baby for Great Yarmouth where she took the room at Mrs Rudrum's. She was almost certainly unaware that her husband was also in the town, staying overnight at the Crown and Anchor, the hotel at which he had earlier spent a weekend with Alice Meadows. This time he had told Alice that he was visiting a sick grandfather in Gravesend. One can only surmise that he travelled to Great Yarmouth to reconnoitre the ground in preparation for the following weekend. Whatever the reason his stay was brief, as he was back in London seeing Alice the next day.

During the following week Mrs Hood came and went from her lodgings, the Rudrums probably assuming that she was keeping assignations with the brother-in-law whom she had mentioned was also staying in the resort. Mrs Rudrum noticed that her lodger regularly wore a gold chain during her stay, and was wearing it on the last evening of her life. Her later testimony to this did much to condemn Bennett.

Mrs Bennett's frequent excursions leads to speculation as to whether indeed she was meeting someone during that week. Certainly Alice Rudrum was later to say in evidence that on the eve of the murder, she had seen and heard Mrs Hood standing outside the house talking to an unidentified man. As Bennett was working on the Friday, and did not leave his Woolwich lodgings until the following afternoon, the question as to the identity of his wife's companion on the Friday evening remains unanswered.

However, Mrs Bennett had been occupying herself during that last week, and it is known that on the Thursday morning she and Ruby were photographed on the beach, with her wearing a chain, and that on the same evening they visited Gilbert's Modern Circus, where they enjoyed watching 'Cleopatra, the Egyptian Serpent Charmer', and 'McCanns troupe of Irish Terriers'. Her husband back in Woolwich was also busily occupied. He called on his wife's former Bexleyheath neighbour on the Wednesday and informed her that Mrs Bennett was in a London hospital; the day after his wife left for Yarmouth, he visited Alice Meadows, and again the following Thursday when he told her that he would not be seeing her on Sunday as was usual as he would be visiting his ailing grandfather again at Gravesend. On Friday he wrote to Alice explaining that he would be going to Gravesend the following day instead of on the Sunday. In fact, on the Saturday, Bennett left work at the Arsenal about midday, went home and changed into a light-grey suit, before setting out to catch the five o'clock train for Yarmouth.

The stretch of beach facing Harboard Crescent is now an amusement park. In 1900 it was a desolate area of sand dunes, grassy hillocks and hollows, favoured by courting couples.

Present there late on Saturday evening, 22 September, a particularly dark and moonless night, was one Alfred Mason, a local youth, and his girlfriend Blanche Smith. Snugly ensconced in a hollow, invisible to anyone passing, they had hardly settled themselves when they heard another couple approaching. They listened as the newcomers sat down about thirty yards away; minutes later Alfred and Blanche were alarmed to hear a woman calling out, 'mercy, mercy', followed by moaning. The young couple, unnerved, had heard enough and got up to leave. As they passed within five yards of the other couple the man, who they saw was kneeling astride a prostrate woman, turned to look at them.

Early the following morning John Norton, a fifteen-year-old local boy was on his way to work when he noticed a woman apparently asleep ...

After spending the night in the Crown and Anchor, on Sunday morning Bennett caught the 7.20 a.m. train back to London.

On arrival he contrived 'accidentally' to meet Alice Meadows in Hyde Park during the afternoon, explaining his unexpected appearance by telling her that his grandfather had been overwhelmed by visitors, rendering his own attendance unnecessary. Later in the week he wrote to inform Alice that sadly his grandfather had passed away on the Sunday morning. In fact the old gentleman was still very much alive as he affirmed in an amusing exchange with the Treasury solicitor at the police court, ' ... are you here to say that you did not pass away on the Sunday, and were buried on the following Tuesday?' asked Mr Wiltshire. 'Yes' was the short reply.

Bennett lost no time in hastening forward his future plans. During the final week of September he called on his late wife's neighbours at Bexleyheath and briefly explained to them that she had been taken ill whilst in Yorkshire. A couple of days later he wrote to the landlord giving three months notice on his wife's behalf. On the last Wednesday in the month he saw Alice, gave her a gold brooch that had belonged to his wife, and persuaded her to agree to bring their wedding forward to Christmas.

Bennett's generosity with his wife's personal belongings continued. A week after the murder, following a casual remark by Alice, Bennett sent her a coat and skirt, a sealskin cape, a silver brooch and a piece of lace, all of which had belonged to Mrs Bennett.

In mid-October Alice gave up her position as a parlour maid at about the time that Bennett showed her their proposed future home at Charlton in south-east London. With Alice's approval he paid an advance on the rent, arranging also for the banns to be put up at her parish church in Stepney. He was unaware that for him time was fast running out.

After weeks of fruitless enquiries, the police achieved the breakthrough they had been seeking. It was a press reporter who first recognized the significance of the number 599 found by Mrs Rudrum on Mrs Bennett's and Ruby's underclothing. Suspecting that it was either a laundry or institution mark, he contacted Detective Chief Inspector Leach of Scotland Yard who had been called in to take charge of the investigation. Leach immediately instituted countrywide enquiries to trace the origin of the mark, a task not made easier on account of the pseudonyms Mrs Bennett had adopted. Eventually the trail led to Kingdom's Laundry, in business at The Broadway, Bexleyheath. It was there soon established that the clothing had belonged to a Mrs Bennett, otherwise known as Hood, and her daughter, both of whom had been living locally.

With the true identity of the murdered woman finally established, the hunt for her killer intensified. Suspicion soon fell on her husband, and police efforts concentrated on finding him. Unaided by modern technology, it was the time-honoured police investigative technique of patient questioning that eventually led them to Bennett's most recent address at Woolwich.

Thus it was that on 6 November, as he left work, Bennett was confronted by Detective Chief Inspector Leach and Sergeant Oldfield, and the hunt for him was over.

At the end of the police court hearing Bennett was committed to Norwich prison to await his trial. A little over three months was to elapse as applications by both the prosecution and defence delayed matters.

During the interim period the nation mourned the death of the Queen. Victoria had reigned for sixty-four years, and the pomp attending her death and subsequent funeral preoccupied the public and the press for many days. However by the time Bennett's trial was due, the nation was emerging from its grief, and was looking to other news.

On Monday, 25 February 1901, Herbert John Bennett stood up in the dock at the Old Bailey against the charge that he had murdered his wife. The trial had been transferred from the Assizes at Norwich to the Central Criminal Court, as the defence contended that the strength of anti-Bennett feeling in Norfolk would prejudice his chances of a fair trial.

Such was the interest in the Yarmouth murder and the subsequent arrest of Bennett that the street outside the Old Bailey on the opening day of his trial was almost blocked by the crowd that had assembled. As at Yarmouth, the majority of those straining to gain admittance to the court were women, most of whom would be unsuccessful and would have to content themselves instead with a glimpse of the accused man as he arrived at court. Those who did manage to gain entry shared every available vantage point not only with each other, but with the corps of press men that were present.

Bennett looked pale but fit, displaying no ill-effects from the weeks he had spent in prison awaiting trial. With his slight moustache waxed at both ends, and dressed neatly in a dark, velvet-collared overcoat with a dark blue silk tie peeping over the top, he looked older than his twenty-one years. He answered clearly, 'not guilty' when the indictment charging him with the murder of his wife was put to him.

Below him Mr Charles Gill, KC, rose to make his opening address. Quiet and persuasive, Gill was one of the most eminent lawyers of the day, a man whose cold, precise logic made him a formidable adversary. His opponent was Edward Marshall Hall, by contrast a flamboyant and histrionic advocate. Whilst Gill would encourage and cajole his witnesses, and would cross-examine those hostile with cobra-like deadliness, ready to strike immediately at a flaw or apparent untruth, Marshall Hall adopted a more dramatic approach, impassioned pleas to the jury typifying his advocacy. For over twenty-five years after the Bennett case Marshall Hall continued as one of the most brilliant advocates practising at the English bar.

Presiding over his first murder trial was Lord Alverstone, the Lord Chief Justice. An impressive figure with a kindly, lugubrious face, very little that was said or demonstrated in court escaped him. He was noted for the protection he gave to witnesses whom he felt were in some danger of being intimidated, a trait not lost on Marshall Hall. Twelve years later he was to preside over a far more notorious trial, that of Dr Crippen and Ethel Le Neve.

As in so many murder trials the evidence in the Bennett case was largely circumstantial. Although there is little doubt that they had been virtual eyewitnesses to the attack, neither Alfred Mason nor his girlfriend Blanche were able to identify Bennett in court.

The prosecution therefore relied on evidence of the movements of the Bennetts before the murder to indicate intent; Mrs Bennett's watch and chain to prove that her husband had been in her company on the last night, and the laundry mark to show how eventually she had been identified. As to motive, the Crown would call Alice Meadows to give evidence of her relationship with the accused.

In his opening speech Mr Gill, after outlining the Bennetts' circumstances since their marriage in 1897, turned to the August bank holiday weekend spent by Bennett and Alice Meadows at Great Yarmouth. The Crown maintained that this visit enabled Bennett to familiarize himself with the resort, by imputation suggesting that he was already contemplating the killing of his wife.

Moving on to the weekend preceding the murder, Mr Gill described how on the Friday Bennett visited both his wife and Alice Meadows. Immediately after her husband's departure, Mrs Bennett went out with a neighbour and 'was buying things obviously with a view to going away'. Bennett was later telling Alice that he would be unable to see her on the Saturday, 'as he had to go to Gravesend on account of the illness of his grandfather'. It is almost certain that instead he travelled to Yarmouth.

Mr Gill continued by reminding the jury of Bennett's known movements during that final seven days. As we have seen he spent most of the week preparing the ground to explain his absence from London during the forthcoming weekend. The movements of his wife in Yarmouth are more obscure. From what little is known it appears that she and Ruby enjoyed a typical week's summer holiday, although there remains a lingering suspicion that she met one or more other men during that week.

Although the prosecution pointed a finger unwaveringly in Bennett's direction, Marshall Hall was undaunted. Under his cross-examination several prosecution witnesses admitted doubt as to the accuracy of some of their earlier testimony at the police court. He rigorously questioned Mrs Rudrum, her daughter Alice, James Conyers, a beach photographer, and Detective Inspector Lingwood as to whether the chain Mrs Bennett had been wearing when she was photographed on the beach was the same as the one found in Bennett's room. Only Mrs Rudrum continued to insist that the chains were identical. Even Lingwood admitted, 'I cannot say what the chain is in the enlarged beach photograph. I cannot judge whether it has links in it ... '

Some light relief was provided when Alice Rudrum confirmed that she had told the inquest that she had seen Mary Bennett standing outside her (Alice's) house talking to a man on the evening of Friday, 21 September (when Bennett was still in London). Although Alice had been unable to see the man, she told the court amid laughter that she had 'heard him quite plainly', as he and Mrs Bennett kissed ... 'I heard the kiss when I had gone away from the window, and when I was standing at the other side of the room'. Despite the amusement her testimony caused, it all proved too much for poor Alice who, after finishing, was seized with a fit of hysterics and had to be carried from the court.

As the usher called out the name Alice Meadows on the afternoon of the trial's second day, spectators craned forward and the eyes of all present turned on her as Alice entered the court and stepped confidently round to the witness box. Dressed in a black skirt, short black jacket and a purple and black trimmed black hat, the image of mourning conveyed was not lost on those present.

In reply to Mr Gill she told the court of her first meeting Bennett, their courtship, engagement and the holidays they had spent together in Great Yarmouth and Ireland. Alice described how Bennett had told her that he was going to visit his sick grandfather on Sunday, 23 September, and how surprised she had been to meet him during the afternoon of that day in Hyde Park. She told of his suggestion that they bring forward their wedding to Christmas, and of the brooch and clothes he had given her. Before the court adjourned for the day, Mr Gill put a final question to her: 'When did you hear of his arrest?' 'On 7 November, the day after he was arrested. Then I learned for the first time that he had been married, and that his wife had had a child.'

The following morning in answer to Mr Marshall Hall, Alice told the hushed court, 'He was kind and gentle, and we gradually got more fond of each other. I became very attached to him, and he behaved to me just as I would have wished in every way. I trusted him ... ' Marshall Hall gently remarked that there was no suggestion of impropriety between herself and Bennett, to which she replied, 'No sir, none whatever.'

Alice stood up well to her ordeal in the witness box, and as she stepped down few, if any of those in court were in any doubt that she had been cruelly duped by Bennett, and was innocent of any complicity in the crime. Despite his duplicity which had now been exposed, Alice gave Bennett a slight smile as she passed him on the way to her seat, the only genuine feeling of warmth extended to him throughout the trial.

Towards the end of the Crown case William Parker, Yarmouth's Chief Constable, Detective Inspector Lingwood of Yarmouth CID and Detective Chief Inspector Leach of New Scotland Yard took their turn in the witness box. Although the Yarmouth officers had devoted a great deal of time and effort to the investigation, at the end of the day they did not emerge with much credit. Detective Inspector Lingwood for example, when searching the dead woman's room at the Rudrums', had overlooked a petticoat with the name Bennett written on it. This was later found by Mrs Rudrum who handed it to the police almost four months later. When asked by the judge, 'Can you explain how the petticoat, which was hanging up on a peg in the woman's room, was not discovered on the morning the search was made?', the unhappy policeman could only reply, 'No my lord.'

The Chief Constable testified that after having escorted Bennett to Great Yarmouth, he was present when Alice Rudrum arrived at the police station and spotted a watch and chain lying on a table which she immediately identified as having been worn by Mrs Bennett. However, under cross-examination Mr Parker was unable to confirm that the chain shown in the beach snapshot was identical with the one that Alice had previously identified; another admission helpful to the defence.

Alfred Leach, the Scotland Yard detective, gave the court details of the enquiries he had made since taking charge of the investigation the previous October, ending by describing Bennett's arrest. This provoked a sharp exchange between himself and Marshall Hall, the latter suggesting that Leach had spoken and acted unprofessionally when arresting Bennett, an allegation strenuously denied by the policeman.

Three other prosecution witnesses are worthy of mention. The first two, William Parritt and John Cameron, Bennett had hoped would provide an alibi for him for the night his wife died. Unfortunately for him, during police questioning both remembered that they had been in his company not on the night in question, but a week later.

The third witness, Alfred Mason, with his girlfriend, had almost certainly been nearby at the time Mrs Bennett was being attacked but had not intervened. Neither counsel made much of this, leaving it to Lord Alverstone to remark scathingly during his summing up that he 'considered it lamentable that through shame or cowardice Mason, when hearing the cries of the unfortunate woman, did not go to her assistance'.

As the trial entered its fourth day nationwide interest was undiminished; crowds still flocked to the Old Bailey, the majority just hoping to catch a glimpse of the leading participants as they arrived or departed.

At lunchtime Alice Meadows walked the few hundred yards to Ludgate Circus where at the ABC restaurant she ate her meal under the curious gaze of a small crowd gathered around the door.

The defence opened its case on the Thursday afternoon, but saved its most sensational witness until the next day. Marshall Hall in his opening speech on Friday morning, first denigrated the press for having 'tried, condemned, and everything short of executed the man Bennett within twenty-four hours of his arrest', and then adroitly manipulated the situation to his client's advantage. The press coverage of the case had, he said, attracted the attention of a man he would be calling as a witness who 'would tell them of one of those extraordinary coincidences, one of those things which, though small in themselves, were important in their effect'.

Mr Sholto Douglas, a fancy box manufacturer in the City of London, was the witness on whom Marshall Hall pinned his main hope of saving Bennett's life.

The witness, who lived in the south-eastern London suburb of Hither Green, stated that he clearly remembered arriving home from work at about 3 p.m. on Saturday, 22 September 1900, and an hour later going out for a walk. During the walk he said he was overtaken by a respectably dressed stranger wearing a grey suit and a bowler hat, who first asked him for a light for his cigarette and then continued uninvited to accompany him.

His companion explained that he was a draughtsman at the Woolwich Arsenal, that he had recently been to Ireland and that he either came from or lived at Bexleyheath. Sholto Douglas was not altogether keen on his new acquaintance, and he later caused some amusement in court when he told Marshall Hall, ' … I could not shake him off … So I asked him to have a drink as a polite way of getting rid of him. He remembered having had a glass of bitter

while the other man had partaken of spirits. Asked by Marshall
Hall how he recollected such detail he replied, 'I know that because
I got sevenpence [3p] change from a shilling [5p]'. As they
emerged from the Tiger Inn according to Sholto Douglas, the man
remarked, 'Oh, a namesake of mine apparently lives there',
indicating the premises next door to the pub which had F.K.
Bennett, Shaving Saloon, over the door. Eventually at 7 p.m. they
parted, the time pinpointed by the witness who said he heard a bus
conductor nearby remark that it was 7 o'clock.

It was in mid-November after reading reports of the Yarmouth
court proceedings that Sholto Douglas said he became convinced
that the stranger he had met, and Bennett, were one and the same
man. The belief prompted him immediately to contact Bennett's
solicitor who made arrangements for him to travel to Norwich
prison.

Marshall Hall: 'Did you see the prisoner?'
Sholto Douglas: I had no doubt that the prisoner was the
man that I met in thelane on 22 September.'
Marshall Hall: 'Have you any doubt?'
Sholto Douglas: 'I have not the shadow of doubt about the
man or the date.'

There was no question that if the jury believed Sholto Douglas,
the prosecution case would collapse. Testimony as to whether Mrs
Bennett had owned one or two chains; evidence of Bennett's and
his wife's movements; his courtship of Alice Meadows – all would
count for nothing, as it would have been impossible for him to
have been in south London at 7 p.m. and in Great Yarmouth, 170
miles away, in time to kill his wife before midnight.

Sholto Douglas was rigorously cross-examined by Gill, but
despite the most probing questions he remained unmoved, sticking
resolutely to the story he had related.

The sensations were still not over. Mrs Cato, a landlady with
whom the Bennetts had at one time lodged at Balham, told the
court that Mrs Bennett had definitely owned two chains, one gold,
the other imitation. She went on to identify the gold chain in court,
while describing in some detail the imitation one. Defence
counsel's satisfaction at her testimony was short-lived, when Mr
Gill extracted from the witness an admission that she had
previously discussed her evidence with a reporter, and that she had

wanted to make things 'as good as I could for Bennett'.

Marshall Hall tried to salvage something from her discredited testimony during his closing speech by bitterly attacking the reporter who had wormed his way into Mrs Cato's confidence and rewarded her impromptu remarks with half a sovereign as a New Year present from the *Evening News*.

The final day of the trial was to start and finish dramatically. No sooner had the court reassembled than Marshall Hall asked leave to call another witness. John Rochfort O'Driscoll, a Lowestoft newsagent, entered the witness box to tell of a dishevelled man arriving at his shop four evenings after the discovery of Mrs Bennett's body, asking for a copy of a paper containing a report of the murder. O'Driscoll had noticed the man's unkempt and agitated appearance, including a boot with a lace missing and scratches on his face and hands. He said he notified the police of the man, but heard nothing further. Like Sholto Douglas it was only after reading a report of Bennett's trial that he had sent a telegram to Mr Robb.

Mr Gill's cross-examination was brief and was aimed at casting doubt on O'Driscoll's conclusions. Marshall Hall alluded to the scratches on the man's face and hands, reminding Lord Alverstone ' ... that the policeman who discovered the body said that there were signs of a desperate struggle having taken place at the spot where it was found'. Mr Gill immediately riposted, 'The doctor's evidence showed that there was no sign of skin under or on the nails of the deceased woman', thus effectively nullifying in one sentence the most significant part of O'Driscoll's testimony.

Bennett's counsel resumed his final speech by dismissively telling the jury that ' ... it was inconceivable that Bennett should commit a murder in a place where he was known'. That Bennett was a proven liar who had led a life of deception was not disputed by his counsel, who wisely decided against calling him to testify on his own behalf, but he attempted to gloss over the lies he had told Alice by claiming that Bennett had only wanted to conceal from her the fact that he was married, an excuse hardly likely to endear his client to the twelve Victorian burghers trying the case.

Point by point Marshall Hall sought to discredit the prosecution case. Evidence that Bennett had been in Yarmouth during the weekends 15/16 and 22/23 September was, he said, dependent upon the testimony of witnesses who were 'unworthy of credence'. He scorned the evidence of William Reade for example, a hotel waiter who gave evidence of Bennett's presence in the Crown and Anchor on the night of 22 September saying it was 'utterly unreliable and untrustworthy'.

Similarly, when referring to evidence of the chain(s), he reaffirmed that in his opinion both the expert evidence regarding the beach photograph, and the discredited testimony of Mrs Cato, pointed indisputably to there being two chains, one having a rope pattern, the other having individual links. Marshall Hall, aware that if the jury took a contrary view his client would hang, pressed home the point. He invited the jury to 'take any opinion they liked, and do what they liked, and he would defy them to get a photograph of the dead woman's chain which would not, in some portion of it, give unmistakable evidence that it was a link chain and not a rope chain'.

Throughout his speech Marshall Hall continued his attacks on the press and the way in which he alleged the newspapers had pre-judged his client. It was fearing possible press interference that had, he said, decided him against revealing until the last minute the presence of so vital a witness as Sholto Douglas.

The defence advocate sat down at 1.15 p.m. after four-and-a-half hours. A section of the press acclaimed 'a sensational speech', an unexpected compliment in view of the attacks he had made upon some of them throughout the trial.

It was now the turn of Charles Gill. He opened his final address by remarking drily to the jury that 'owing to Mr Marshall Hall's speech it appears to be necessary to bring your minds back to the case presented on behalf of the prosecution.' This he went on to do during the next two-and-a-half hours. Devoid of the posturing that was characteristic of his opponent, Gill relied solely upon an extended left forefinger to emphasize his arguments.

He pointed out that from Bennett's position it was essential that Alice Meadows be kept in ignorance of his wife and child's existence, and this could most effectively be achieved by disposing permanently of his wife, while leaving the authorities with the problem of Ruby's welfare. Gill repeatedly urged home the point that no satisfactory account of Bennett's whereabouts during the two crucial nights of 16 and 22 September had been advanced by the defence. If he was not in Great Yarmouth, where was he?

The watch, and more particularly the chain Mrs Bennett had been wearing on the night she died was again the subject of comment and speculation. 'How, why and when,' he asked, 'had Bennett been given his wife's watch and chain?'

One by one the Crown advocate refuted the issues raised in Bennett's defence. Whereas Marshall Hall had played upon the jury's emotions, Gill relied upon their commonsense response to the logic of his arguments. Fact after fact he introduced with the intention, as he put it, 'of clearing the cloud of gloss spread over the case by the brilliant rhetoric of my learned opponent'. He disposed almost contemptuously of the evidence of Sholto Douglas, linchpin of the defence case. 'It is strange that the prisoner had not mentioned the incident of his meeting with Mr Douglas which was of the greatest importance to him ... ' 'No person ever saw Mr Sholto Douglas in the company of the prisoner, and every statement he made was matter that could have come to his knowledge through reading the particulars published in the papers ... ' 'The whole story was amazing and extraordinary and absolutely opposed to every fact in the case'.

Gill described Bennett as 'a designing man who thought and planned that which would further the objects on which he was at the moment engaged'. Bennett's wife, he suggested, 'had under his instructions lived a life of false representation'. As he listened to Gill's condemnation, Bennett for the first time during the trial was overcome with emotion. Two warders moved closer as his head dropped below the level of the dock rail, and for several minutes he seemed affected by the stress of his situation. When eventually he raised his head, the strain and anxiety which he had so far concealed was reflected in the anguish shown in his eyes. He nevertheless managed a wan smile, as if to apologize for his lapse.

Finally Gill sat down. After his closing admonition to the jury that, 'if they were not satisfied with his case it was their duty to acquit the prisoner, but if they were irresistibly forced to the conclusion from the accumulative evidence that the prisoner had murdered his wife they must not shrink from discharging their duty in bringing in a verdict of guilty', there were few in court who would have been prepared to forecast the final outcome. For Bennett the ordeal was still not over; the judge, Lord Alverstone, had yet to sum up.

The summing-up was a flawless example of conciseness and objectivity. Speaking in a low, carefully modulated voice, his body half-turned so as to face the jury, and occasionally referring to his notes, the Lord Chief Justice reviewed the evidence. Whilst ensuring with scrupulous fairness that everything in the accused's favour was brought to the jury's attention, he nevertheless clinically demolished most of the defence case.

That the Bennetts had led a dishonest and amoral life together was not disputed, but the judge instructed the jury to ignore it and to concentrate solely on facts relating to the matter before them. After dealing briefly with the evidence of Mason and his girlfriend, Lord Alverstone concisely reminded the jurors of the circumstances leading up to the murder. How the Bennetts' marriage, initially happy, deteriorated, and how matters were precipitated after Bennett had met Alice Meadows in the summer of 1900. By the time he and Alice became engaged, it was clear that his wife presented a tiresome and seemingly insuperable obstacle to their continuing romance.

The judge drew attention to the defence assertion that Mrs Bennett had permanently left Bexleyheath in mid-September 1900, her departure being mutually agreed with her husband. The fact that she had departed without mentioning to her neighbours that she was leaving permanently, that she left behind her personal valuables and trinkets – but took the key to her home – he suggested mitigated against the defence submission.

Considerable significance was attached by Lord Alverstone to the letter allegedly postmarked Woolwich and addressed to Mrs Hood at the Rudrums'. 'If the jury arrived at the conclusion' said the judge, 'that the letter came from the prisoner at Woolwich, it was an important piece of evidence against the prisoner, as showing that he knew his wife was at Yarmouth.' Similarly, the judge pointed out, the lies Bennett had told Alice Meadows as to his whereabouts on 15 and 22 September suggested that he had no desire for her to be aware of his movements on either of those two Saturdays.

As Lord Alverstone continued, Bennett listened intently, only the occasional tug at the waxed ends of his sparse moustache betraying his anxiety. His hopes were momentarily raised when His Lordship advised the jury that if they believed the evidence of Sholto Douglas it would be an end to the case, only to be dashed when he qualified his remarks by saying that it was very dangerous to rely upon such uncorroborated evidence.

Lord Alverstone went on; had Bennett slept at his lodgings on the night of 22 September, he asked. There were witnesses who had testified under oath as to his presence in Great Yarmouth. If his wife had gone to Great Yarmouth without his knowledge, the subsequent disposal of her clothes and jewellery was of little significance. If on the other hand the jury took the view that he knew only too well what had happened to his wife, his subsequent action was indeed material.

Near the end of his summing-up, when referring to the watch and chain worn by Mrs Bennett at Yarmouth, Lord Alverstone said that if the jury was satisfied that they were identical to those found later in Bennett's room, it was very strong evidence against him.

The jury retired at 6.40 p.m. and a mere thirty-five minutes later they filed back into court to deliver a verdict of guilty.

When asked by the clerk why sentence of death should not be passed upon him, Bennett replied in a firm voice, 'I say I am not guilty, sir.' He leaned almost nonchalantly on the front of the dock as Lord Alverstone sentenced him, apparently oblivious to the faint sound of cheering from the crowd outside the court as news of the verdict reached them. He then turned and walked briskly from the dock on his way to the condemned cell at Norwich prison.

Poor Alice Meadows; she had remained in court after having given her testimony. As soon as the verdict and sentence had been pronounced, she was helped from the court sobbing uncontrollably, to collapse outside. Her world had disintegrated. The innocent maiden who had fallen for the blandishments of the young deceiver had now to go and face the world again, forever tainted in her own eyes with the knowledge of her frailty and gullibility.

A crowd later gathered outside the office of the *Eastern Evening News* in Lowestoft where the trial's result was displayed in the window. An early edition was quickly sold out, and by the time an 'extra special' edition arrived later from Norwich, the crowd had grown to several hundred. Traffic was diverted, and not surprisingly a plate glass window of the newspaper office gave way under the press of people. As they swarmed in clutching their halfpennies, and clamouring for a copy of the paper, a second window was smashed, and at one stage the entire office front was at risk of being demolished. Women fainted, and several other people were crushed and bruised before the pressure gradually subsided, as the crowd drifted away leaving behind men and women's hats, a shredded topcoat and an assortment of feathers, handkerchiefs and other personal oddments.

Bennett was to remain in the condemned cell for almost three weeks awaiting execution. During this time he was by all accounts a fractious prisoner, making difficult the unhappy task of the warders assigned to watching him. Meanwhile, Marshall Hall, still believing totally in his client's innocence, was making strenuous, but in the end unavailing efforts to win him a reprieve.

Shortly before eight o'clock on the morning of Thursday, 21 March 1901, a small group entered Bennett's cell. Asked if there was anything he wished to say, his short, defiant reply was 'no confession'. A few minutes later as the black flag was hoisted over the prison to signal his execution, the mast snapped and fell to the ground. It was suggested by some that this was a divine sign; was Marshall Hall right after all?

*Postscript:*

Eleven years after the execution of Bennett, on 14 July 1912, Dora May Gray was found strangled on the beach at Great Yarmouth with a bootlace around her neck. Her murderer was never found.

# 2   The Bath Chair Bombing, Essex 1943

The stark facts surrounding the death of Archibald Brown in July, 1943, are recorded on Essex County Police form R1175/130: Crime Report reference 1396/B21 dated 11 January 1944, as follows:

> Deceased's son, Eric James Brown, obtained 'Hawkins 75' grenade mine from military store during course of his military duties, and whilst on leave, placed it in the seat of father's invalid chair. Deceased was being wheeled by nurse when there was an explosion, killing him and seriously injuring the nurse.

Parricide, the killing of one's parents, is a comparatively rare offence that normally arouses greater revulsion than almost any other kind of murder, with the possible exception of child slaying. When Eric Brown decided to kill his father in the summer of 1943, by exploding an anti-tank mine under his wheelchair, the perpetrator and the method adopted forged a uniquely lethal combination.

Nowadays with the proliferation of terrorist attacks, bombings have become relatively commonplace. Not so in 1943; although the country was in its third year of war, the urban populace was only accustomed to hearing explosions resulting from enemy air raids. This case was very different; the blast which had literally blown forty-seven-year-old Archibald Brown to pieces, critically injured his nurse Elsie Mitchell and damaged nearby property, had originated beneath the cushion of Mr Brown's wheelchair.

In the summer of 1943, the tide of battle was at last turning in favour of the Allies. In July, Sicily was invaded, the prelude to a long, bloody but ultimately successful Italian campaign, while in Russia the war of attrition was continuing with the launching by the Red Army of a massive counter-offensive in the direction of Orel, a hundred miles south of Moscow.

Back at home the population were determined to enjoy the summer despite rationing, air raids (although these were diminishing), and other wartime irritations. Nearly 15,000 visitors crowded into Southend during the weekend of 24/25 July, taking advantage of the resort being one of the few in the south of England not having a ban on trippers.

Those who opted to remain at home could hear of the war's progress from no less than twelve Home Service and Forces news bulletins (including one in Welsh), while in a lighter vein listeners could enjoy *Music While You Work*, Jack Payne and his orchestra, or the band of the Irish Guards.

It is doubtful if either indoor or outside pursuits held much appeal for the occupants of 19, London Hill, Rayleigh, that weekend, following the sudden and violent death that had befallen the head of that household on the Friday.

The chain of events that had culminated in Mr Brown's untimely end in mid-July, 1943, could be traced back to an unhappy marriage that somehow had survived for twenty years. Three years before his marriage Archibald Brown had sustained serious injuries in a motor-cycle accident. He seemed to recover, but the long term effect of his injuries may well have influenced his later behaviour. For the next fifteen years his humiliating and brutal conduct towards his wife and eldest son made their lives unbearable.

Excessive and unreasonable domestic demands, curtailing the freedom of his wife Dorothy to visit friends and family and constant verbal abuse became the established pattern of their married life. Similarly, with his eldest son, his sadistic and boorish behaviour led to years of torment for the boy. Only his younger son, Colin, three years Eric's junior, escaped Mr Brown's wrath.

When he was eleven years old Eric went to boarding-school, thus being delivered from his father's malign influence, but who knows but that the seeds of his future mental disorder had not already been sown.

In 1938 further disaster overtook the family when Mr Brown was struck down by spinal paralysis, resulting in him losing the use of both legs. His condition deteriorated until by the time of his death five years later he was confined to his bed and to an invalid chair. Concurrent with his physical decline had been an emotional backlash directed against his wife. His attitude and behaviour towards her became even more intractable, with calls for assistance becoming ever more frequent and demanding.

In 1940 Eric left school and started work in Barclays Bank, where his behaviour at times was decidedly odd; although for most of the time he reportedly worked efficiently, he was prone to brainstorms whereby he would fling his arms into the air and then beat a rapid tattoo with his fists on his desk. When to this behaviour was later added a minor fraudulent transaction, the bank decided that enough was enough, and although not prosecuted, Eric was asked to resign.

The year 1942 was a milestone in Eric Brown's life. He attained the age of eighteen and so became eligible for service in the armed forces. In October he was duly called up into the army. Like so many other young men at that time he probably felt that at last he could cast aside the shackles of home. Although the future was uncertain, at least it held the promise of some excitement. Above all he was free, or so he believed, of his father's endless persecution.

After completing his basic training, Eric found himself with the 8th Battalion, the Suffolk Regiment, at Spilsby in Lincolnshire. There is nothing to indicate that he was anything other than a good soldier. Being an infantryman his training included lectures and demonstrations by Sergeant S.F. Smith, a battalion weapons instructor, on the mechanism and correct use of small arms and mines, including one known as the 'Hawkins 75 grenade mine'.

While Eric settled down to army life, back home nothing had changed. His mother was still being subjected to her husband's tyrannical behaviour, which had got even worse since his eldest son had left home, fuelled as it was by his almost total physical immobility.

Eric had hoped to put his past unhappiness behind him after joining the army, so he was dismayed to receive a letter from his mother in the spring of 1943, informing him not only of his father's deteriorating physical condition but plaintively recounting the continuing ill treatment and abuse she was still suffering at his hands.

In May and June he spent three weeks leave at home during which he witnessed again the treatment of which his mother complained. When Eric Brown departed at the end of his leave in June to return to his unit, the youth who for so long had himself suffered wretchedly at his father's hands, and who now bore witness to his mother's daily unhappiness, had decided that the time had arrived for him to put an end to the suffering of both his parents. By now convinced that his father too was the hapless victim of the crippling illness that had struck him down, Eric came to the conclusion that by eliminating Mr Brown senior, he would not only release his mother from her distress but would also deliver his father from his suffering. The questions remaining were when and how he was to achieve his object?

Military camps, by the very nature of their existence, frequently have large stocks of various weapons within their boundaries. In wartime this proclivity is greatly increased. In 1943, Spilsby in Lincolnshire, where Eric Brown was stationed, was no exception. Included among a variety of small arms and other weapons held by the unit were 200 anti-tank mines of a type already mentioned, the 'Hawkins 75 grenade mine'. Eric decided that a weapon capable of disabling an enemy tank or armoured vehicle should prove more than adequate for the more modest but equally lethal requirement he had in mind. So it was that without any great difficulty Eric acquired such a mine, an ignitor and a detonator, all of which he secreted in his attaché case. As he had anticipated, their disappearance passed unnoticed.

During Eric's leave in June Mrs Brown had unknowingly hastened her husband's demise by writing to her son's Commanding Officer, Captain J.L. Bell, requesting that he be granted compassionate leave. Ostensibly the reason was to enable Eric to find someone to run his father's business, but one suspects that Mrs Brown was in truth hoping to have her eldest son at home, at least for a time, to support her in coping with her disabled and vexatious husband. Her request was considered sympathetically, as a result of which in July Eric found himself back home again, this time for three full months.

He arrived home on the 12th to find the domestic situation unchanged. His father was his usual rancorous self, while Mrs Brown still submitted to her husband's every demand. Their eldest son spent the eleven days following his return home working in his father's mill which adjoined the house. He also found time to disappear into the family air raid shelter in the garden where he busied himself modifying the grenade mine he had brought home with him. The simple expedient of removing four corner supports from beneath the pressure plate allowed the plate to rest directly on the body of the mine, thus requiring far less pressure than was normal for it to detonate. Having satisfied himself that the device was functional, all was now ready for him to put his plan into execution.

Apart from his wife, Mr Brown had a nurse ministering to his needs. Elsie Mitchell was the third who had taken on this responsibility, and it would seem that she was better-liked and more highly regarded by her patient than had been her predecessors.

One of the regular duties she undertook when the weather was fine was to take Mr Brown out for a walk in his wheelchair – the only outing he was by this time still able to enjoy. So it was that on Friday, 23 July 1943 Nurse Mitchell went to fetch her employer's wheelchair from the air raid shelter in the garden where it was usually kept. She was puzzled to find the shelter bolted on the inside, so after trying unsuccessfully for a few minutes to open the door, she went to summon Mrs Brown to assist her. When the two women returned, they were startled when the door of the shelter opened suddenly and Eric emerged. All three were momentarily taken aback and Eric, confused and evasive, replied that he had been 'looking for something', when asked by his mother his reason for being there.

Eric then disappeared indoors, while his mother and Nurse Mitchell took the wheelchair back to the house where Mr Brown was waiting, dressed in his pyjamas and dressing gown. After he had been helped into the chair and warmly wrapped in a travelling rug and blanket, two pillows were positioned behind him. Elsie Mitchell then set off with her charge. The couple were passing Rayleigh church when Mr Brown fumbled in his dressing gown pocket trying to reach his cigarettes. Nurse Mitchell stopped and moved round to the front of the chair to help him; after lighting his cigarette, she returned to the rear of the wheelchair to continue their journey. She had scarcely moved off again when Mr Brown shifted himself in the chair to settle himself more comfortably ...

'There was a terrific bang. I felt hot at my feet and legs, and my hair smelt burnt'. So Elsie Mitchell later described the instant that her patient had been hurled into eternity. That she had not accompanied him was attributable solely to the pillows and cushion in the wheelchair that were between herself and the source of the explosion. As it was those first on the scene found the nurse unconscious and with terrible leg injuries. Of her charge there was no sign until someone noticed a human leg suspended in a nearby tree, and a torso lying in the road. The remainder of Mr Brown's dismembered body was soon discovered nearby.

Whilst Nurse Mitchell was rushed by ambulance to Southend Municipal Hospital, Police Sergeants Gowers and Pattison, Constable Leggett and Air Raid Warden Fuller made a preliminary search and examination at the scene. They noticed that the road surface was pitted with a number of small holes and they recovered several small pieces of metal that were lying nearby.

Once it was learnt that no enemy aircraft had been in the vicinity at the time, explosives experts were summoned. They took little time in reaching the conclusion that the explosion had taken place between the seat and axles of the wheelchair. This was later to be confirmed by Dr J.M. Gilmour, who examined what remained of Mr Brown. Furthermore, two of the pieces of metal found were identified as having been part of an anti-tank grenade mine.

It was now established beyond doubt that Mr Brown's death had resulted from a deliberate act, rather than from an accident of war. The Essex CID, who had been informed and who had kept abreast of developments, now became fully involved, with Detective Inspectors Draper and Barkway setting the investigation under way. A few days later, upon returning from leave, Detective Superintendent G.H. Totterdell took over.

'Tot' Totterdell, the son of a country police sergeant, had joined the Essex police force in 1912. After service in the Royal Naval Air Service and the Royal Air Force during the First World War, he returned to the police and became a CID officer in 1921, rising to become the county's first Detective Superintendent in 1931. A quietly spoken, grey-haired man, Totterdell over the years had acquired the attributes that form part of every successful detective's make-up; patience, doggedness, an unfailing eye for detail and a sixth sense which often prompted him to pursue a particular line of enquiry when less tenacious colleagues would have been satisfied with their initial impressions and conclusions. This last ability was to prove useful during the 'Rayleigh Bath Chair' case as it became known. As the investigation advanced numerous statements were taken from witnesses and others whom it was thought may be able to throw some light on the enquiry, including the dead man's widow. Mrs Brown made what appeared to be a comprehensive statement, but after reading it Totterdell was left with the feeling that she was holding something back.

Nonetheless Mrs Brown's statement contained sufficient background information about her marriage and her late husband's behaviour to persuade Totterdell and his colleagues that her son Eric warranted further and more detailed investigation. This was to prove rewarding; during the following days detectives checked and verified the facts Mrs Brown had supplied. They also came up with further interesting information concerning Private Eric James Brown of the Suffolk Regiment. They found out from his unit that he had received instruction in the operation of anti-tank mines, but also more ominously they learnt that he had access to the mine store and would have had no real difficulty in obtaining one.

By this time enquiries among friends, neighbours and relatives of the Browns had confirmed Archibald Brown's treatment of his wife and son over the years.

Back in Rayleigh experiments with a similar wheelchair to that used by Mr Brown confirmed that a mine, suitably modified, could be placed beneath the seat cushion and would remain unnoticed by the chair's occupant. When sat upon in precisely the correct position the device would detonate with predictable results. By the time the evidence had been collated and assessed it was mid-August, and Totterdell was satisfied that Eric Brown, the dead man's eldest son, had had the motive, the means and the opportunity to kill his father.

Totterdell decided to hold a conference of all those involved in the investigation, where after some discussion it was agreed that the next step should be a further interview with the suspect.

Totterdell sat looking at the boyish-faced, bespectacled youth sitting opposite, wondering how he would respond to the questions about to be put to him by himself, and Inspectors Draper and Barkway, who were also present.

The Superintendent had wasted no time after the conference the previous day in having Brown brought to Rayleigh police station for more questioning. He started by asking him to explain his presence in the air raid shelter on the afternoon his father died. Brown's reply was non-committal and evasive. The detectives persevered, all three in turn probing with their carefully phrased questions, hoping for a response that was contradictory, self-incriminatory or indicative of the suspect's innocence. It was a slow, devious process, and by lunchtime little progress had been made.

Totterdell invited his two colleagues to go and partake of lunch, leaving him alone with Brown. After Draper and Barkway had left the room, it seemed that Brown's reluctance to discuss his father's death lifted. He chatted more freely to Totterdell, telling him of the family unhappiness over the years that had led to his decision to kill his father, and describing the method he adopted. When Draper and Barkway returned he quite readily agreed to Totterdell's suggestion that he make a written statement. This was written down by Detective Inspector Barkway, and it clinched the case against the suspect. Part of it read;

' ...For this last four-and-a-half years, and even before that, life has ceased to exist for my mother but has become a complete drudgery as a result of my father's treatment to her. I decided that the only real way in which my mother could lead a normal life, and for my father to be released from his sufferings, was for him to die mercifully.' He ended his statement, 'My father is now out of suffering, and I earnestly hope that my mother will now live a much happier and normal life. This I declare is the only motive I had for bringing about my father's death ... '

After signing the statement, Eric Brown was formally charged with the murder of his father on 23 July at Rayleigh.

Brown made two appearances at Southend Petty Sessional Court before he was committed for trial on 20/21 September. In the meantime there was an interesting development, when Mrs Brown sought out Superintendent Totterdell to volunteer another statement. Totterdell had felt all along that her first statement had not told the whole story; his instinct was now to be proved correct. Now that her son had been arrested and charged, Mrs Brown no longer felt the need to protect him. She therefore made a second, much fuller statement, detailing her late husband's treatment over many years not only of herself, but of his eldest son. It was a distressing story that helped to explain her son's state of mind during the last weeks of her husband's life.

The committal proceedings lasted for two days. Brown was represented by Mr J.P. Nolan, while the case for the Crown was in the hands of Mr J.F. Claxton. After outlining the events of 23 July, and calling Nurse Mitchell to describe the final moments leading up to the explosion, Mr Claxton called Mrs Brown to the witness box. In answer to his question she described how ' ... during the last two years I was unable to do anything right for my husband. Occasionally he would tip his tea over me, and, when irritated he would grab my clothes and pull me down ... ' She added that she had no doubt that her son was aware of these happenings. In answer to Mr Nolan she agreed that although her husband had treated Eric badly as a child, since the onset of her husband's illness five years earlier father and son had been on good terms. This was a direct contradiction of what she had told Superintendent Totterdell a few days previously.

Mrs Brown ended by telling the court of the worsening treatment she had received at Archibald Brown's hands during the last four months of his life. At the end of her testimony the prosecution had established a motive for the murder that however inexcusable was to many of those listening at least understandable.

By the end of the second day's hearing Mr Claxton had called his other witnesses, including Sergeant Smith, the battalion weapons instructor, who told the court, 'Since about 15 January I have been instructing soldiers. My syllabus included lectures on British mines, and on 21 April last I gave a lecture on No 75 grenade mine and others. The accused should have attended this lecture, but I could not swear that he did so'. Perhaps more importantly, Sergeant Smith could not swear that Brown did *not* attend the lecture.

Others, expert and non-expert alike, gave their evidence. They included Dr Gilmour, the pathologist who had examined Mr Brown's remains, Captain Bell, the Commanding Officer of Eric Brown's unit, who testified as to his being on compassionate leave at the time of the murder, and explosives experts called upon to describe the nature of the device used, the apparent modifications that had been made to it by the accused and its effect when detonated. Police Sergeants Gowers and Pattison, Constable Leggett and Warden Fuller, who each described the scene as he found it very soon after the explosion, and finally, Detective Inspectors Draper and Barkway and Superintendent Totterdell, who between them gave details of the police investigation, including the final interrogation of Brown.

At the conclusion of the prosecution case, Mr Nolan reserved his client's defence, while the court chairman, Mr W.G. Rainer, committed Eric Brown for trial at the Essex Assizes.

The trial of Eric James Brown took place at Chelmsford and lasted for only one day, Thursday, 4 November 1943. On a day that the newspapers carried reports of the heaviest raid yet by the USAAF on the German North Sea port of Wilhelmshaven; of an enemy air attack on East Anglia resulting in a number of casualties; instructions from the Ministry of Food on how to make an omelette for two out of 'reconstituted' dried egg, and finally that the black-out commenced at 5.51 p.m, Brown stood in the dock and pleaded not guilty to the murder of his father. Mr Cecil Havers, KC, for Brown, made no attempt to deny that his client had indeed caused the wilful death of Archibald Brown. His defence was based solely on Brown's state of mind at the time – did he know what he was doing, and if so did he know he was doing wrong?

Sir Charles Doughty, KC, after outlining the evidence that had been tendered at the committal proceedings, called Detective Inspector Barkway to the witness box. Cross-examined by Mr Havers, Barkway told the court that his enquiries had established that there was insanity in the Brown family. He also recalled the strange behaviour of Brown when he had earlier been employed by Barclays Bank.

Dr Rowland Hill, a neurologist and psychiatrist called by the defence, said that he had reached the conclusion after examining Brown whilst he had been on remand that he was suffering from the early stages of schizophrenia. 'He would have a wholly distorted idea of what he was doing,' the doctor said. He went on to say that at one stage he asked Brown why he had done this thing? He answered vaguely and then said, 'if someone had been standing by my side to tell me what would have been the result of my action, I would never have done it.' He then burst into tears.

To rebut the evidence of Dr Hill, the prosecution called Dr R.G.Lyster, the medical officer at Chelmsford prison. He stated that having seen and spoken to Brown every day since his admission to the prison hospital on 21 August, he had come to the conclusion that he was sane. The doctor added that 'the only thing that might be regarded as an indication of insanity was that on 25 October he endeavoured to commit suicide by cutting his neck with a knife'. Dr Lyster thought that it had been 'a genuine attempt, but it was not a very serious wound'.

The jury came to the conclusion that brainstorms, the blowing up of his father and the cutting of his own throat could hardly be regarded either singly or collectively as the acts of a rational man, and after retiring for three quarters of an hour they returned a verdict of 'guilty but insane'. Mr Justice Atkinson forthwith ordered that Eric Brown be detained until His Majesty's pleasure be known.

Thus ended a tragic case that attracted little attention from the press of the day, preoccupied as it was with more world-shattering events.

That Eric Brown was insane, there is in my view little doubt. Whether the insanity was hereditary, or arose as the result of his unhappy childhood, allied to the years of distress he had experienced at witnessing the unholy treatment his mother had suffered at his father's hands, is arguable. Dr Hill indicated that the latter was the case when he said that Brown was suffering from the early stages of schizophrenia. Detective Inspector Barkway, on the other hand, testified that he had established that there was insanity in the Brown family.

Wherever the truth lies, one cannot help feeling after so many years a certain sympathy for a young man, not yet twenty years of age, who after years of suffering at his father's hands was so confused and distraught as to see the death of his father as the only answer. The method he chose to end his mother's continuing unhappiness had drastically and effectively ended also the life of his father. Perhaps only his son realized that not only was Archibald Brown the victim of a crippling physical disease but was undergoing mental torment greater than his own.

# 3   The University Killings, Cambridgeshire 1930

The sight of a man staggering out of Gibb's Building next to King's College Chapel, Cambridge, on a warm summer's day in June, 1930, drew the attention of passing staff and undergraduates alike. Curiosity quickly turned to alarm as the man collapsed to the ground and gasped out, 'He shot me.' Whilst some tended him, others hurried into the building where they found the study door of Alexander Wollaston, senior tutor at the college, wide open. A horrifying sight met the gaze of those who cautiously entered the room. Wollaston lay spreadeagled beside an overturned chair, while beside him lay a young man, blood spreading from beneath his head.

Cambridge University in 1930 was largely insulated from the problems besetting the rest of the country. The depression, unprecedented unemployment, and the realization by men who had survived the Great War that the nation had not turned out to be the promised Utopia, were matters of transitory concern to dons and undergraduates alike, with only a few exceptions. Immersed in study and research, the majority of the middle and upper-class undergraduate population confined their social life also to the university campus, where societies and clubs catering for a wide range of intellectual, political and sporting tastes proliferated.

Some ventured forth to the city pubs and cinemas, and at the weekend punting on the River Cam was a traditional pursuit. Few went further afield, trips to London and other large towns being confined to vacations when study, tutors and examinations could be temporarily forgotten whilst enjoying the latest West End show or film. In short, university life in 1930 provided not only intellectual stimulus, but a wide enough range of social, leisure and sporting activities to satisfy all but a few nonconformists.

Such an individual was Douglas Newton Potts, a nineteen-year-old freshman from Sevenoaks in Kent. Tall, slim and aesthetic-looking, he had come up to Cambridge with an open scholarship from Lancing College in Sussex to read history, and was by all accounts a brilliant scholar.

Notwithstanding this, during his first year he was not enamoured with either the academic or social life at the university. With the exception of a jazz band he had formed in which he played the drums, he avoided university extra-curricular activities. He and a small group of friends preferred to visit local hostelries in the Cambridge area where, posing as a Russian prince, he informed anyone who cared to listen that a member of his entourage was heir to the Russian throne. This masquerade fooled no one; as Nancy Williams, a local publican's daughter, said later, 'Potts was a very nice boy, but terribly eccentric.' This was an apt description, and it seems that he was regarded with the tolerant amusement the local inhabitants reserved for the more crack-brained schemes and behaviour indulged in by some of the undergraduate population.

None of this would have mattered had not Potts run into debt, owing money both to friends at the university, and to local shopkeepers. Having a less wealthy background than many of his contemporaries, but nevertheless determined to keep up appearances, his allowance from home fell short of his requirements. His borrowing started in a small way: 2/6d. (12½p) from his immediate friends, a few shillings 'on the slate' at a shop, rapidly escalated until by the time he went home for the Easter vacation he owed a lot of money and demands for repayment were assailing him from all quarters.

In May 1930 Alexander Frederick Richmond Wollaston, a tutor at King's for less than two years, had already established a reputation among dons and undergraduates alike as a com-passionate and kindly man. They could take their problems to him and be assured of a courteous reception and an attentive hearing, followed by carefully considered and well balanced suggestions as to their solution.

He had an affinity with King's, having been an undergraduate there himself. Now over thirty years later at the age of fifty-five, he was overjoyed at being back and having the opportunity to dispense to the young men following in his wake some of the wisdom he had acquired from his experiences during the intervening years. And what a wide range and quality of experience he could draw upon. After leaving Cambridge where he had read medicine, he built up a reputation during the pre-war years as a notable explorer and naturalist. His journeyings to remote parts of the world resulted in several books in which he described his adventures and findings.

During the First World War he was awarded the Distinguished Service Cross whilst serving as a surgeon in the Royal Navy. Afterwards he returned to his travels. He was on the 1921 Mount Everest expedition, and later was climbing again in a remote area of Colombia. Between-times he got married, and at the time of his death he and his wife had three children.

So to 1928, and the invitation to become tutor at King's. He had no hesitation in accepting, and after being duly elected he took up his appointment in 1929. The Dean of King's, the Reverend Milner White, was later to say of Alexander Wollaston, 'He was a very great and good man, one of the most famous explorers living'.

Meanwhile during the early summer of 1930, the man of whom the Dean spoke was becoming increasingly concerned over the wayward behaviour of one of his freshmen, Douglas Newton Potts.

The third participant in the approaching tragedy was a thirty-six-year-old policeman, or to be precise, Detective Sergeant, in the Cambridge Borough Police Force. With ten years service, five of which had been in the CID, Francis James Willis had already received several commendations for bravery, and seemed destined for further advancement in his career. A married man, but with no children, he, like Wollaston, had served in the war, in the army with the 2/5th Suffolks and the 4/3rd King's African Rifles.

On Tuesday, 3 June 1930, Willis was informed that an undergraduate who had been missing from King's College for ten days was returning from London. As he held a warrant for the young man's arrest, Willis decided to go along to Fitzwilliam House, where he was due to arrive with friends and meet him. Douglas Newton Potts was the undergraduate's name.

When Potts left home to return to Cambridge at the end of the Easter vacation in 1930, his father felt happier than he had done for some months. During that period his son had written to him several times telling of his shortage of money, and asking for help in paying off some of his more pressing creditors. Potts senior had helped him, but remained very concerned at his son's apparent inability to manage his finances at the university.

He and his wife were therefore pleasantly relieved when during the Easter holiday their son discussed his future at Cambridge, and assured them that henceforth he would apply himself assiduously to his studies, with a view to eventually making the law his career.

The letter they received a few weeks later from Alexander Wollaston, explaining that Douglas had absented himself from the college without permission for three days, and that no one knew of his present whereabouts, must have come as a profound shock. After failing himself to contact his son, Mr Potts agreed that the university authorities should notify the police.

In fact, when Douglas Potts returned to Cambridge after Easter, far from applying himself to his studies he embarked upon the course that was to end so disastrously a few weeks later.

One of his first acts was to steal a .32 Webley automatic pistol from a fellow undergraduate who owned the weapon quite legitimately. Potts was unable to resist showing the gun to a confidant named Newman, a like-minded young man who played the trumpet in his band. Newman agreed enthusiastically when his friend suggested that together they embark on a life of crime, and himself went straight out and bought a revolver.

At first, although both were now lethally armed, they continued as before. They managed to buy a second-hand motor car between them in which they travelled round Cambridgeshire frequenting public houses. In these, after adopting fictitious titles, they regaled other customers with impressive but fanciful stories of their property, wealth and imaginary exploits. Few people took them seriously, although they may well have done had they known of the loaded gun each was carrying.

Both young men lived in a world of fantasy, boosting each other's self-esteem, and dispensing mutual support and admiration for the more inventive schemes each dreamed up. Possibly they were influenced by the lurid newspaper and cinema newsreel accounts of the current gang warfare in the United States. If so, no evidence exists that either of them ever tried to emulate the exploits of the mobsters across the Atlantic.

Before long their money started to run out. They sold their car and bought a cheaper motor cycle, but Potts continued to be hounded for money he owed. They decided that the only solution that appealed was to leave Cambridge permanently and make their way to London. So it was that on Saturday, 24 May 1930, after loading what little they could on to the carrier of their motor-bike, they set off southwards determined to try their luck away from the cloistered environs of the university.

Upon reaching London they sold the motor cycle for twenty pounds, a worthwhile sum in 1930 and sufficient for them to survive on for a few days. They stretched it as far as they could by sleeping rough. During the days they wandered aimlessly, aware of the need to conserve their money, and as the week progressed they already questioned the wisdom of their decision to leave Cambridge.

During the Thursday night, five days after their arrival, it rained. This added to their despondency and dimmed even more the glittering hopes they had held less than a week before.

Prior to leaving Cambridge a fellow undergraduate had provided them with the name and address of a young woman acquaintance who, he assured them, would help if the need arose. As both Potts and Newman by now were fed-up, besides being cold, wet and hungry, with no shelter or work and very little money, they decided to call on Madge Miller at her Shaftesbury Avenue flat.

Ostensibly Madge was employed as a dancing instructress at a night-club, but this may well have been a euphemism for a rather more lucrative but equally sociable occupation. Be that as it may, true to their friend's word, she evinced no outward surprise either at their unexpected arrival halfway through the night, or at their sorry appearance. She invited them in, made them a pot of tea and let them flop exhausted into the first proper bed they had experienced since leaving Cambridge. They were pleasantly surprised to be awoken in the morning by a maid who brought them tea in bed.

After having rested, dried out and tidied themselves up, the spirits of Potts and Newman rose, and some of their earlier optimism returned. During that Friday they went out to search vainly for a man whom Potts said would help them financially. Eventually Potts ended up by selling his cuff-links. This provided enough money to enable them to take Madge out on the town that evening, during the course of which they wined and dined, visited a cinema and later a show. Not surprisingly, by the time they returned to the flat their money was spent.

Potts and his companion almost forfeited Madge's goodwill when later that night she discovered the guns they still possessed. She was experienced enough to know that young men in their situation, dependant upon her hospitality, may well decide that desperate measures were required to alleviate their difficulties. If those measures involved the threatened use of firearms, she knew that dire results could ensue.

Her composure was hardly restored by Potts' remarks and behaviour during the next few days. He reverted to his earlier fantasizing, telling her of money he had borrowed from a Russian friend, who happened also to be heir to the Russian throne, and also, much closer to reality, that warrants for his arrest were in existence in connection with some questionable financial transactions. When Potts and Newman waved their guns about and threatened to shoot themselves, Madge probably reflected on the imprudence of having taken in, albeit unknowingly, two such capricious young men, mentally resolving to rid herself of them as soon as she could conveniently do so.

Meanwhile, Potts and Newman were out pawning further items of jewellery to enable them to stay solvent. On Saturday Potts wrote to an undergraduate friend of Newman's at Cambridge called Bolton, thanking him for having lent them some money and enclosing the pawn ticket for Newman's watch as security against the debt. He also asked him to send his dress suit to Post Restante, Charing Cross post office, addressed to Stephen Morris, a name he assumed for the purpose.

That night they went out to a cinema together for the last time with money that Madge had borrowed, added to that which Potts had obtained from a pawnbroker; by Sunday they were broke again. On the Monday, after some discussion together with gentle urging from Madge, Potts and Newman finally left the Shaftesbury Avenue flat. Although sorry in some ways to see them leave, as for most of the time she had enjoyed their company, Madge also felt relieved at their departure as there was a certain unpredictability about them, particularly Potts, that had frightened her.

For the two young men, they were back where they had been four days earlier. All day Monday they wandered around the London streets, and that night they again resigned themselves to sleeping out in the open. At least on the morrow they would have some money, after collecting Potts' dress suit and pawning it.

On Tuesday morning they made their way to Charing Cross Post Office. As they entered the building a shock awaited them; there standing by the counter was Bolton and his friend.

When Bolton had received Potts' letter he had debated on what to do. He was aware that both Potts and Newman were missing from their respective colleges and that neither would wish for his whereabouts to be made known to the university authorities – the assumed name to which he was to address the parcel confirmed this. On the other hand, would it not be better for them to be hauled back now, when there was perhaps an outside chance that they would not be sent down, rather than to delay matters until such a fate was inevitable? In the end he had shown the letter to his own college authorities, who had asked him to try to persuade the two recalcitrant undergraduates to return. He had confided in a friend, who had agreed to accompany him in his car to London.

To the relief of Bolton and his companion, neither Potts nor Newman raised any serious objection to the suggestion that they should return to Cambridge. Their woebegone appearance indicated that a hot bath followed by a rest would best fit them for their forthcoming confrontation with the university authorities.

Bolton drove straight back to Fitzwilliam House, the college to which Newman, himself and his friend belonged. There Potts left them to walk back to King's on his own. It was not far, Fitzwilliam House in 1930 being situated opposite what is now the Fitzwilliam Museum in Trumpington Street. (The present Fitzwilliam College, as it is now called, dates from 1966 and is a mile beyond King's College, across the River Cam and on the Huntingdon Road.)

It was a surprise to both Potts and Alexander Wollaston when the two met, and as they walked back towards their college together it is reasonable to assume that they started to discuss Potts' absence, a discussion that they would continue when they reached Wollaston's study. Neither of them was probably aware of the man following them. It was Detective Sergeant Willis, who had been waiting outside Fitzwilliam House for Potts to arrive back from London.

The police had been kept informed by the university of developments since Potts' letter had been received, so Willis planned to meet the young freshman upon his return to execute a warrant for his arrest.* The policeman had intended to apprehend his man at Fitzwilliam House, but when Potts left his companions to walk back to King's, Willis probably decided that it would be

---

* The precise nature of the warrant is not known, but it seems likely that it related either to a road traffic accident in which Potts had earlier been involved, or to one of his dubious financial transactions.

more expeditious to follow and speak to him in private rather than in the street. Soon after Wollaston and Potts had disappeared into the college, the detective approached the porter's lodge and asked to be directed to the tutor's study. Potts and Wollaston had hardly settled themselves before there came a knock at the door, and in response to Wollaston's invitation Willis entered the room.

He introduced himself to both men before turning his attention to Potts. He explained his presence, and had started to tell him that he was being arrested, when suddenly without warning the young man produced a pistol. He fired first at Willis, wounding him in the shoulder, before turning to his tutor who was stumbling backwards over his chair. Two more shots erupted, killing instantly the man who had survived the worldwide perils of mountains, jungles and war, only to return to the haven of the college he loved to meet a violent, bloody end.

Potts had not quite finished; he fired again at Willis, this time as it turned out, fatally, before pressing the muzzle of the pistol to his own head and squeezing the trigger. The detective, still conscious, managed to stagger to the outer door before collapsing.

Both Willis and Potts, who was still alive, were rushed to Addenbrooke's Hospital. Potts survived for just over four hours, dying at six o'clock the same afternoon. Willis lingered for another twelve hours, eventually succumbing to the second bullet wound the next morning.

News of the unprecedented tragedy stunned university and town alike. Speculation and rumour abounded, but only gradually did the full story and background of the harrowing series of events emerge.

That Douglas Potts was an eccentric who lived largely in a make-believe world, can reasonably be accepted. But what changed him from being a harmless oddball and dreamer into a double killer is far harder to understand and evaluate. There was no evidence of a psychopathic disorder; on the contrary he was an inoffensive young man, given to fantasizing, but quite averse to violence. I am convinced that at the time he stole the Webley pistol he had not the slightest intention of ever using it, and that his proposal to Newman that henceforth they should lead a life of crime together was another example of his desire to impress others.

I would suggest a more straightforward explanation. That Douglas Newton Potts, nineteen-year-old Cambridge freshman from Sevenoaks, suffered a brainstorm. After leaving the university with Newman ten days before, vowing never to return, there he was, chastened and dispirited, facing the imminent prospect of being sent down to return in disgrace to his family, his ephemeral dreams of making good in London shattered.

But let us suppose that during their short walk together back to King's he had gleaned some slight hope during his conversation with Wollaston that perhaps all was not entirely lost; that genuine remorse and promises as to his future behaviour may yet retrieve the situation and avoid him being sacked from the university. Having no sooner arrived in Wollaston's study, and when about to discuss the matter further and try to enlist his tutor's sympathy and support, they had been interrupted by the arrival of Willis to arrest him.

In an instant his slight hope of a reprieve was overturned. Trouble with the police leading almost certainly to a court appearance, on top of his current problems would, he knew, inevitably result in him being sent down. But he still had the gun; blast the policeman, and Wollaston, and himself, and the whole damned lot of them ... with that he fired the first shot.

# 4   Who Slew Rose Harsent?, Suffolk 1901

Few people would argue that before the abolition of capital punishment for murder in the United Kingdom the ultimate ordeal a person could undergo was to stand trial for his or her life. A hung jury and a subsequent retrial must have been an even more nightmarish experience. Such was the anguish to which William George Gardiner was subjected in November 1902 and January 1903, when he stood accused at Ipswich of the murder of Rose Harsent, a twenty-three-year-old servant girl.

At the turn of the century Peasenhall was typical of countless other villages throughout the land. The workforce, almost to a man, was employed on the land or in some associated agricultural industry, represented in Peasenhall by Messrs Smythe & Sons, manufacturers of farming implements at the Drill Works. The womenfolk were either at home or working as servants at the homes of the more prosperous inhabitants in the neighbourhood. The nearest town of any size was Saxmundham, a pleasant five mile journey by pony and trap, while excursions to Ipswich entailed an extended journey by rail.

Religion figured prominently in the lives of the villagers. Besides the parish church of St Michael, there lay just across the boundary, in the adjoining village of Sibton, the Primitive Methodist chapel. It was two members of the chapel's congregation who were to occupy centre-stage in the drama that was to unfold in the summer of 1902.

The village inhabitants were parochial in their outlook – unless one of the village sons was fighting, what concern of theirs was the war in South Africa? They busied themselves with their own affairs, and often with those of their neighbours. Very little that took place in a village of some seven hundred souls passed unnoticed.

It was against such a backcloth that there occurred the events for which an explanation is as remote now as it was over eighty years ago.


In May 1901 William Gardiner, tall, swarthy and heavily-built, with a full beard and moustache to complement a head of thick black hair, was thirty-four years old and at his prime. Highly regarded in Peasenhall, he worked as a foreman at the Drill Works, where his skill and reliability earned him enough to keep his wife Georgina and their six surviving children comfortably in their three-bedroomed cottage. Most evenings he spent at the Primitive Methodist chapel; besides being the Sunday school superintendent, he was an assistant steward and the choirmaster, all posts that enhanced his reputation in the village.

It was therefore with disbelief that the villagers greeted the news that two village lads had one evening seen Gardiner and a young female member of the choir, Rose Harsent, entering an old thatched building known as the 'Doctor's Chapel', situated just off the main road. Not content with that, the two youths had crept up to the chapel wall and eavesdropped on the naughty conversation and shameless activity that they later alleged had ensued.

When news of the alleged incident became public knowledge it provoked an immediate reaction. Gardiner summoned the two young men, George Wright and Alphonso Skinner, before him and demanded an apology. This was not forthcoming, both of them sticking to their story.

The Primitive Methodists decided to hold an enquiry into the allegations. Held under the auspices of John Guy, Superintendent Minister of the Wangford circuit, the enquiry failed to reach a conclusion as to the truth or otherwise of the allegations. Nevertheless, Gardiner felt it incumbent upon himself to offer his resignation from the various offices he held. However, as the enquiry members had no authority to accept his resignation, and in view of the outcome of the enquiry, the matter was allowed to drop.

What of Rose Harsent at this time? A twenty-three-year-old domestic servant whose parents lived in the village, while she herself lived and worked at Providence House, she was an attractive girl with her fair share of admirers. Although found to be pregnant at the time of her death, I would hesitate to assume that because of this lapse she was necessarily a promiscuous young woman. Indeed at Gardiner's trial, Mrs Crisp, her employer's wife, was asked by defence counsel, 'If you believed this girl was an immoral young woman, you would not have kept her?'

'No, I should not', was the reply.

Rose's employer, William Crisp, a retired tailor, was also deacon at the Doctor's Chapel, while his wife Georgina was a member of the chapel congregation. Rose, although not a congregationalist, cleaned the chapel every week. She did not appear at the Primitive Methodists' enquiry, perhaps fearing that she would be intimidated and embarrassed when interviewed by several of her fellow villagers about her alleged indiscretion. She agreed, however, to see John Guy in her mother's presence a few days later, and to him she completely denied the allegations made by Wright and Skinner.

Gardiner and Rose no doubt hoped that this was the end of an unhappy and sordid episode, and that they would each be able to resume their lives as before. Unfortunately matters were not to be so easily resolved; Gardiner may have suspected as much when shortly after the enquiry John Guy spoke to him privately and in effect warned him that in future his behaviour would have to be beyond reproach. He assured Guy that he would do everything possible to restore himself fully in the eyes of his neighbours.

During the next twelve months rumour and innuendo persisted, suggesting that the association between Gardiner and Rose was by no means over; on one occasion Gardiner received an anonymous letter advising him again as to his behaviour, but the author, who revealed himself at Gardiner's first trial, was later discredited.

Despite Gardiner's repeated assertions that nothing improper ever took place between himself and Rose Harsent, poor Rose still found herself to be pregnant in the spring of 1902. Her condition, it was suggested, provided the motive for her murder, the father of the unborn child not wishing for his involvement to be publicly exposed.

Excitement was in the air throughout the land during the last week of May 1902. For two weeks the news had been that peace was imminent in South Africa, that after two-and-a-half years the conflict that had cost the lives of 22,000 imperial and colonial troops was coming to an end. The hopes of the population were not misplaced; the peace negotiations that had been carried on at Vereeniging culminated in the surrender terms being signed at Pretoria on Saturday, 31 May.

The country was also looking forward to the Coronation of King Edward VII, due to take place on 26 June. Newspapers were devoting considerable space to advertisements for illuminations, fireworks, decorative glassware and countless other items on a coronation theme, unaware that the ceremony was to be postponed until 9 August, due to the King's sudden illness.

For the cricket lover the last weekend in May 1902 was to be disappointing; the storms that had been sweeping the country had saturated the ground at Edgbaston during the Friday night, thereby restricting play on the last day of the test match against the Australians to one-and-a-quarter hours. The match predictably fizzled out in a draw.

The rain was soon to reach East Anglia, one of the worst storms in living memory raging over the region during the night of Saturday, 31 May/Sunday, 1 June, villagers, their faces illuminated by lightning, standing at their windows or front doors involuntarily flinching as the thunder crashed and grumbled its way overhead, while for hours torrential rain lashed down, transforming the main street into a deluge.

Gardiner was one of those who chose to stand by his front door to watch the storm's progress. Just after ten o'clock he had a few words with Henry Burgess, when, like Burgess, he possibly noticed the light gleaming from the top window of Providence House, two hundred yards down the road.

Later during the night Gardiner and his wife joined Mrs Rosanna Dickenson, their next-door neighbour, to keep her company while the storm lasted.

Across at Providence House Mrs Crisp was suddenly awakened by a thud and a faint scream, but after being reassured by her husband that Rose would come to their room if frightened by the storm, she turned over and went back to sleep. Outside the tempest continued to rage.

Sunday morning dawned bright and sunny. As the church clock of St Michael's was striking eight William Harsent was approaching Providence House. Every week his routine was the same; a walk to the house to take his daughter Rose change of clothes and freshly laundered underwear. He strode round the back, through a small conservatory at the rear and into the kitchen ... He stopped short, appalled and sickened by what he saw. Lying on the kitchen floor in her nightdress and stockings, her head near the stairs and her feet beneath where he stood, lay his daughter. At a glance he took in the pool of blood which had spread from the two gaping slashes across her throat, and the burn marks on her nightdress. Automatically he bent down and covered her body with a rug and moved part of a broken paraffin lamp away from her, before turning to stumble outside. There he met James Crisp making an early call on his brother William at the house. After glancing briefly into the kitchen, Crisp joined Rose's father in hastening off to summon aid and to notify the authorities.

Almost eight months were to pass before Gardiner stood in the dock at the Suffolk Assizes at Ipswich, for the second time accused of Rose Harsent's murder.

It was an eventful period for all concerned, from the time Eli Nunn, the Peasenhall village constable, arrived at Providence House at twenty minutes to nine on Sunday morning, 1 June 1902, until twelve minutes past seven on the evening of Saturday, 24 January 1903, when the foreman stood up in court to deliver the jury's verdict.

PC Nunn's enquiries had led him to call at Gardiner's home on the Tuesday evening following the murder with a warrant for his arrest for the murder of Rose Harsent. Gardiner's response had been to tell Nunn, 'I am not guilty.' Further enquiries by Nunn and Superintendent George Staunton resulted in the accumulation of evidence, as a consequence of which on 30 June the Coroner's jury brought in a verdict of murder, naming William Gardiner. Three days later at Saxmundham police court the magistrates committed him in custody for trial at the next Suffolk Assizes, due to start on 7 November.

The first trial of William Gardiner for the murder of Rose Harsent took place at Ipswich between 7 and 10 November 1902, before Mr Justice Grantham (Sir William Grantham). Leading the case for the Crown was Mr Henry (later Sir Henry) Dickens, son of the famous novelist, later to distinguish himself as Common Serjeant of the City of London. Lean and hawk-faced, Mr Dickens was one of the most able and distinguished advocates of his time, as gifted in his chosen field as had been his father in the literary world. As his junior counsel he had the Hon. John de Grey.

Opposing him was Mr Ernest Wild, a much younger and less experienced barrister, but one who nonetheless was to give notice of his future brilliance by his defence of Gardiner. At the time of the Gardiner trials he was a junior on the south-eastern circuit, but

like Dickens he later rose to the judicial bench, becoming Sir
Ernest Wild, Recorder of London. A well-built, distinguished-
looking young man, he was a brilliant orator, and although on
occasions inclined to pomposity he nevertheless exuded genuine
charm, a valuable asset for any advocate. He had Mr H. Claughton
Scott as his junior.

Both Mr Dickens and Mr Wild, with their respective juniors,
were to contest Gardiner's second trial. Only the judge differed,
Mr Justice Lawrence presiding instead of Mr Justice Grantham.

This account of the Peasenhall murder confines itself to the
second trial. Suffice to say in respect of the first, that after the legal
battle had been fought over four days the jury were unable to
agree, and Gardiner was remanded back in custody to await a
retrial.

It is almost impossible to imagine Gardiner's feelings as he
awaited his second trial. As his counsel Ernest Wild later said in his
opening address, 'What the strain upon his nerves must have been
it is impossible for any human being to conceive.'

As mentioned, with the exception of the judge, the lawyers
involved the second time were as before. Mr Justice Lawrence,
(The Honourable Sir John Compton Lawrence), former MP, one
time Recorder of Derby and leader of the Midland circuit, had
been a judge of the King's Bench Division for twelve years. His
pugnacious appearance belied a benevolent nature. Despite any
other misgivings he may have had, William Gardiner could rest
secure in the knowledge that his trial would be presided over by
one of the most astute legal brains in the country.

As was usual with well-publicized murder trials, the County
Hall at Ipswich was besieged by hundreds of people on
Wednesday, 21 January 1903, all of them hopeful of gaining
admittance to the opening day of the second Peasenhall murder
trial. Again only a few were successful, priority being given to
nationwide press representatives.

Gardiner appeared in the dock, soberly dressed in a black suit,
and showed little emotion throughout the duration of the trial,
apart from when his wife was testifying on his behalf.

Mr Dickens stood up and commenced his opening speech by
advising the jury to disregard all that they knew and had read
about the first trial, and to concentrate their minds solely on the
evidence that this time was to be put before them. He then
introduced the prisoner, described the layout of Providence House,

and outlined the circumstances surrounding the Doctor's Chapel incident, and Gardiner's alleged subsequent behaviour.

He continued by summarizing the evidence he intended to introduce, during the course of which he referred to the motive the Crown ascribed to the murderer. 'Then there is the girl in the family-way – six months gone. Someone in Peasenhall must have had an interest in getting rid of the girl, because no one can suggest that this murder was committed for gain or for robbery or for jealousy. It was for the object of getting rid of the girl, and if possible of destroying the body'.

The question for the jury to decide was whether or not William Gardiner was the person who had 'got rid of the girl'.

George Wright and Alphonso Skinner, who were called early on in the proceedings, corroborated each other's evidence. After describing what they said they had heard taking place between Gardiner and Rose Harsent in the Doctor's Chapel on 1 May 1901, they were cross-examined by Mr Wild. Wright admitted that he had been reprimanded by Gardiner at work, and perhaps more significantly that some five years earlier he had circulated similar rumours about a young couple he had seen in his mother's orchard. Skinner told Mr Wild that both the doors and windows of the Doctor's Chapel were shut at the time that he and Wright were outside.

John Guy, who had presided over the chapel inquiry, in telling Mr Dickens of what had transpired at the inquiry referred to Gardiner's unimpeachable character, and his offer to resign from his chapel offices. He mentioned that he had spoken privately to Gardiner after the inquiry, when he said the latter had admitted his indiscretion in having on occasions accompanied Rose home, a very minor transgression as Guy admitted to Mr Wild.

Henry Rouse, a seventy-three-year-old labourer and a lay preacher at the Primitive Methodist chapel, appeared to those present to be a vindictive, self-righteous old man. After admitting that following the chapel inquiry he had continued to monitor Gardiner's behaviour, he told of remonstrating with him after seeing him walking with Rose one evening, saying that Gardiner had immediately promised him there would be no repetition. This was a conversation that Gardiner later strenuously denied ever took place. Rouse's credibility took a battering when he admitted sending an anonymous letter to Gardiner rebuking him after supposedly having seen him sitting in the chapel choir stalls during a service, with his feet resting on Rose Harsent's lap.

Mr Wild ruthlessly cross-examined Rouse, accusing him of having in the past made an unsubstantiated allegation of arson against a twelve-year-old boy, of having had an affair with a former employee's wife, and finally of having made scurrilous allegations against a neighbour's daughters. Rouse vehemently denied these charges, and although unable to substantiate them in court, the details Mr Wild had revealed were sufficient to plant doubt in the jury's mind as to the truth of Rouse's testimony, and to cause speculation as to his motive for giving evidence.

The last witness on the first day of the trial was Mrs Georgina Crisp, the occupier of Providence House, who told the court of being awoken by a thud and a scream during the night of the murder. She had not gone to investigate the source of the disturbance, and able only to estimate the time it occurred as between 1 and 2 a.m. This was unfortunate for both sides, as if the time Rose was killed could have been accurately fixed it would have been simple enough to establish whether or not Gardiner could have been at Providence House at the material time. For some unknown reason neither side called William Crisp, the person who may have been able to throw some light on the matter.

The second day of the trial was mainly devoted to police and medical evidence. Before then several villagers testified; Rosanna Dickenson, the Gardiner's next-door neighbour, told of how they had kept her company during the storm. James Morries told of having seen distinctive footmarks leading to and from Gardiner's cottage to Providence House during the early hours of Sunday, 1 June, and John Rickard, secretary at the Drill Works, spoke of the general availability in the works office of the buff coloured envelopes in which Gardiner was supposed to have enclosed his letters to Rose.

The stolid figure of Peasenhall's village constable, Eli Nunn, entered the witness box and took the oath. He described how he had found Rose lying on her side with burns to her body and nightdress. Lying on the floor nearby had been a burned out candle, a broken paraffin lamp and a broken bottle, on the label of which was written 'Two or three teaspoonfuls, a sixth part to be taken every four hours – Mrs Gardiner's children'.

Upstairs in Rose's bedroom he had recovered a number of letters, including two sent to her by Gardiner at the time of the Doctor's Chapel incident in 1901, and a letter of assignation received by her on the eve of her death. This read, 'D.R. I will try to see you tonight at 12 o'clock at your Place if you Put a light in your window at 10 o'clock for about 10 minutes then you can take it out again don't have a light in your Room at 12 as I will come round to the back.' Nunn also found letters, described by the prosecution as 'of a grossly indecent character', written and sent to her by Frederick Davis, her young next-door neighbour. The constable finished by telling of his visits to Gardiner's home before and after his arrest to interview Mrs Gardiner, and to retrieve items of her husband's clothing.

In answer to Mr Wild, Nunn admitted that initially upon arriving at Providence House he had thought Rose's death to be suicide. 'I did not think of anything else. Of course after seeing the wounds and finding the letter it made me think of something else,' he said. The policeman also related the conversations he had had with Mrs Gardiner; during one of these she had told him that some time before she had given Rose Harsent some camphorated oil, after having first decanted it into a medicine bottle.

Nunn was followed into the witness box by his senior officer, Superintendent Staunton. He had questioned Gardiner about the letters found in Rose's bedroom, and his wife regarding his movements on the weekend of the murder. He told Mr Wild that his first reaction was also that the death was a suicide. Staunton was further cross-examined about three 'confessions' that had come into police hands. Although one of these had warranted an in-depth investigation, it had been finally established that there was no truth in any of them.

After the police came the medical evidence. Dr Charles Ryder Richardson had carried out the post-mortem on Rose and described the wounds to her neck, one of which had completely severed her windpipe. He went on, 'There were numerous semi-circular cuts about her hands, most of which were caused by upward blows such as in warding-off blows,' thereby ruling out the possibility of the injuries having been self-inflicted.

Dr Charles Edward Lay had attended the scene on the Sunday morning and had made the preliminary examination of the body. The witness had concluded that death had occurred at least four hours earlier. He also had removed from the broken bottle the label he had previously written giving dosage instructions for Mrs Gardiner's children.

Finally a Dr Stevenson, senior Home Office analyst, told the court that apart from a minute speck of blood of indeterminate origin found between the handle and blade of a knife, he had found no other such traces on Gardiner's clothing or shoes.

Before the prosecution case ended, young Frederick Davis underwent a torrid examination at the hands of both counsel about the letters he had written to Rose. 'Do you know these verses get more and more filthy as they go on?' asked Mr Wild at one stage. 'Yes,' admitted Davis miserably. The letters caused acute embarrassment to their author, but advanced not at all the case for either the prosecution or defence.

The final prosecution witness at the end of the second day was Thomas Gurrin, a well-known handwriting expert who later in the year was to testify at the trial of Samuel Herbert Dougal. Asked by Mr Dickens for his opinion as to whether business letters admittedly written by Gardiner were in the same hand as the letter of assignation received by Rose Harsent on the eve of her murder, Gurrin replied, 'To the best of my belief these documents that I have been comparing were all written by the same hand.' Notwithstanding his conviction, under cross-examination Gurrin's replies were punctuated by reservations about the conclusions he had drawn, thus illustrating to those present that graphology at best was an imprecise faculty.

On Friday, 23 January 1903, the third day of William Gardiner's second trial, his counsel Mr Ernest Wild rose to open the defence case.

After a confident address during which he critically analysed the prosecution evidence, he ended by appealing to the jury to find Gardiner 'not guilty of the atrocious charge which had unjustly been brought against him', before calling his first witness, Mrs Georgina Gardiner, wife of the accused man.

A small, frail woman who answered the questions put to her with quiet dignity, she recalled without difficulty the events on the murder weekend eight months before. How she and her husband had kept Mrs Dickenson company from between eleven and eleven-thirty on the Saturday evening, until half-past-one on the Sunday morning. How later that morning after breakfast, her husband had taken their children to Sunday school. She went on to tell of the subsequent visits by PC Nunn, Superintendent Staunton and other officers, and their questioning regarding her husband's movements during the crucial weekend, the broken medicine bottle found lying on the kitchen floor near Rose's body and the Doctor's Chapel allegations of 1901. On the Tuesday evening the police had again visited them, and after taking possession of most of William's clothes, had arrested him for Rose Harsent's murder. Mrs Gardiner said that the police had continued to call on her on one pretext or another for the next five days, the visits only ceasing after she had spoken to Mr Leighton, her husband's solicitor.

As the court rose for lunch at the end of her testimony, she fainted, and had not recovered sufficiently to undergo cross-examination when the court reassembled in the afternoon. It was therefore agreed that the prisoner should next be called.

Gardiner appeared relaxed in the witness box. Smartly dressed, his hair and beard neatly trimmed, he rested his hands on the side of the box and awaited the questions from his counsel. When he spoke his voice was unexpectedly quiet, so much so that he was several times asked by Mr Wild to speak up. After describing the events of 1 May 1901, and emphatically denying the version given by Wright and Skinner, he told of his later conversation with them in his office when he had challenged their allegations. He also told the court of what had transpired at the subsequent inquiry.

He unhesitatingly answered questions put to him regarding the letters that had passed between himself and Rose Harsent. These he said, had related to chapel matters, and in May, 1901, to the allegations made by Wright and Skinner. Mr Wild then referred to the knife which Gardiner admitted he had formerly possessed. He said the speck of blood that had been discovered on it was from rabbits that on occasions in the past he had disembowelled and skinned.

His advocate moved to the night of 31 May 1902. He examined Gardiner's movements, commencing with his arrival home from work on the Saturday evening and ending with him taking his children to Sunday school the next morning. Gardiner explained that he and his wife had been in Mrs Dickenson's from before midnight until one-thirty on the Sunday morning, and that he had gone to bed about half-an-hour after returning home. His wife, he said, had got up twice during the night, the first time to comfort their young son Bertie who was crying, and on the second occasion to go downstairs for some brandy as she had stomach ache. He had not left the bedroom until he rose at eight o'clock.

Gardiner went on to answer with conviction the searching questions that were asked of him by Mr Dickens in cross-examination. 'Had you any knowledge whatever of the death

of Rose Harsent until you heard of it in going to Sunday school?',
was Mr Dickens' opening question.

'No,' replied Gardiner.

The Crown counsel hearkened back to the events surrounding
the Doctor's Chapel allegations in 1901. 'Now we come to Rouse,'
he said. 'Is Mr Rouse's story a fabrication from beginning to end?'

'Yes.'

'Not a word of truth in it?'

'No.'

'Is it untrue that you were walking with a girl late at night?'

'It is.'

Again when referring to Gardiner's interview with John Guy
after the chapel enquiry, Mr Dickens asked, 'Is it true you told Mr
Guy you would keep clear of young women generally, and of Rose
Harsent in particular?'

'No; I did not.'

'Anything of that kind?'

'No; because I had no reason to keep clear of Rose Harsent,'
Gardiner replied.

Speaking of Wright and Skinner, Gardiner was equally positive.
When Mr Dickens pointed out that after starting the Doctor's
Chapel story they had stuck to it at the enquiry, he told him, 'It was
compulsory then, for they could not go back from it; if they had
done they would have been hooted from the place.'

'Can you suggest any ill-feeling in either of these two boys
against you?', asked Mr Dickens. 'Not until this scandal, and then
they were forced to stick to it, and there has been ill-feeling ever
since, and there always will continue to be.'

Later Gardiner spoke up on Rose's behalf when he was asked,
'With regard to Rose Harsent, you never saw her guilty of any
impropriety of conduct?'

'I cannot say I have never seen her walking with anyone, but I
can say this, I have never seen anything improper between her and
other men.'

Mr Dickens was unable to make any significant inroad into
Gardiner's account of his movements during the night of the
murder, and soon afterwards ended his cross-examination.

The general feeling in court was that the accused man had
acquitted himself well. He had remained unruffled, and his
answers to questions put to him by both advocates had been
unequivocal and to those listening had appeared truthful.

After Gardiner had returned to the dock, there followed several defence witnesses who either corroborated what had been said on his behalf, or rebutted prosecution evidence. James Fairbank and Herbert Bayliss, both senior bank officials called to counter the evidence of Thomas Gurrin, were subjected to a trenchant cross-examination by Mr Dickens, who questioned their professed graphology expertise. Martha Walker, another Primitive Methodist, was only briefly in the witness box, but her testimony in Gardiner's support was forthright and was untouched by Mr Dickens short cross-examination. Finally, before the court adjourned at the end of the third day, several elders of the Sibton Primitive Methodist chapel entered the witness box to vouch for Gardiner's unimpeachable character.

There was a delay in the start of the proceedings on the fourth and final day of the trial. A Mr Noel Etheridge told the court that when he had gone to collect Mrs Gardiner from her lodgings she had been seized by a fit of 'high stericks'. In reply to Mr Justice Lawrence who asked, 'Is she in the town?', Mr Wild assured him,

'She shall be brought, ill or well', before peremptorily instructing that a doctor be sent at once to see the nervous and reluctant woman.

The doctor's attendance seemed to have had the desired effect, as Mrs Gardiner arrived not long afterwards and took her place in the witness box. Wearing a dark dress relieved by a bright red blouse, her nervousness was plain to see as she awaited her delayed cross-examination.

To her relief Mr Dickens' questioning was at first innocuous. Later his approach changed imperceptibly, and his questions were more loaded. 'What time did you suggest you went to Mrs Dickenson's that night?' he asked.

'About half-past eleven, I should say,' she replied.

'Am I right in saying you told the police: "We went at eleven and stopped till half-past one?" '

'I did not say to the police the exact time. I said from eleven to half-past. I told them my husband came shortly after, the same as I told you when I gave my evidence at the last trial.'

'Half an hour afterwards?' pressed Mr Dickens.

'No, a very few minutes after.'

'Do you mean he almost followed you in?'

'I told you what he did. He went upstairs to look at the children.'

The prosecuting counsel's covert suggestion that Gardiner, by not immediately following his wife into Mrs Dickenson's, had allowed himself time to have gone to Providence House, killed Rose and returned within half-an-hour, had been effectively countered by Mrs Gardiner. Mr Dickens moved on to a different tack.

'Rose Harsent of course was constantly at your house?'

'Not constantly; she came when she liked,' Mrs Gardiner parried.

'You never saw her guilty of impropriety with any man?'

'No.'

'Of course, if your husband had walked out with her, you did not know it?'

'My husband never did walk out with her.'

'You cannot say that, but of course you believe in your husband?'

'Yes, I do,' said Mrs Gardiner loyally.

She was briefly re-examined by Mr Wild who asked her finally, 'You had believed in your husband?'

'Yes.'

'You still believe in him?'

'Yes, I do,' she replied.

As she left the witness box it was agreed that despite her obvious and understandable apprehension, she had, like her husband, stood up well to her ordeal. For his part it was noticed that Gardiner had difficulty in controlling his emotions while his wife was testifying.

The trial now entered its final stage, with only counsels' closing speeches and the judge's summing-up remaining.

Mr Wild spoke first, a notable speech to which even his opponent later paid tribute. While unashamedly playing upon the jury's emotions, ... 'are these poor helpless children to be branded for all time as the children of a man who has committed such a dastardly crime?', he at the same time attacked the prosecution case. He cleared of any involvement in the crime both the writer of the anonymous confession that had been closely scrutinized by the police, and Frederick Davis, author of the 'filthy' letters found in Rose's bedroom. Davis's relief at being publicly cleared of suspicion was short-lived, as Mr Wild suggested, albeit on the flimsiest of evidence, that he was the father of Rose's unborn child.

The scandal allegations of 1901 had been effectively disposed of at the Sibton chapel enquiry he said, so he made only a brief, disparaging reference to the evidence of Wright, Skinner and

Henry Rouse. Similarly with the handwriting expert Thomas Gurrin. Mr Wild asserted that the prosecution had been obliged to fall back on his supposed expertise after the other matters upon which they depended had either been effectively countered or discredited.

Gardiner's advocate reminded the jury of Mrs Martha Walker's brief testimony in which she had spoken of Gardiner's respectability, had corroborated his wife's explanation as to how the labelled medicine bottle had come to be in Rose Harsent's possession and had exposed the spurious evidence of Henry Rouse. Little wonder that Mr Wild told the court, 'I attach the very greatest importance to the evidence of Mrs Walker.'

After referring to the improbability of Gardiner having been able to commit the murder without his wife's knowing, and without there being left a vestige of blood on his clothing, his counsel devoted much of the remainder of his speech to eulogizing his client's integrity and devotion to his family, and Mrs Gardiner's honesty and loyalty. He finally sat down with the words, 'Gentlemen, my duty is done', his task completed.

When Mr Dickens rose to address the court, he set out by reminding the jury that it should not allow misplaced sympathy for Mrs Gardiner to influence its decision … 'there is hardly a crime which is committed which does not bring unhappiness, grief, sorrow and ruin upon the relatives of the guilty man', he said.

He then entered into a lengthy criticism of the defence tactics. These included the introduction of last-minute witnesses without notifying the opposition, whilst objecting to the prosecution doing likewise; over-emphasis of the piety and the esteem with which Gardiner was held in Peasenhall; and the reference by his opponent in his opening speech to the anonymous 'confession', which, according to Mr Dickens, was introduced solely to divert suspicion from Gardiner.

The prosecutor contended that an accumulation of small facts, including his access to buff envelopes, the shoemarks to and from his cottage to Providence House and his need, assumed by the prosecution, to prevent his paternity of Rose Harsent's expected baby from becoming public knowledge, pointed irresistibly to Gardiner's guilt. He vigorously defended the prosecution witnesses, particularly the discredited ones, but, in attributing to Henry Rouse a friendly, protective role towards Gardiner, adding that the anonymous letter he had sent was 'couched in most considerate language', Mr Dickens surely taxed the credulity of his audience to the limit.

Moving on to the night of the murder and subsequent events, the Crown's case assumed a more formidable aspect. Morries' testimony as to the shoemarks; Gurrin's opinions on the handwriting differences and even Gardiner standing at his front door, according to Mr Dickens to check whether a light was showing from Rose's bedroom, all seemed more ominously significant as he expounded upon them.

He questioned the veracity of Mrs Gardiner's statement that she had been awake until five o'clock on the Sunday morning, after having risen at seven the previous morning. Her husband's evidence he dismissed in a sentence: 'With regard to Gardiner himself, of course if you disbelieve his story about Rouse you cannot trust a word of his evidence.'

Mr Dickens ended with a final adjuration to the jury, 'Gentlemen, you have shown great attention to this case; I am sure you will give effect to your conscientious belief, and your conscientious belief alone.'

There remained the summing-up of Mr Justice Lawrence. After explaining to the jury the difference between direct and circumstantial evidence, he carefully reviewed everything put before them during the four days of the trial.

Commencing with the Doctor's Chapel incident of 1901, and the evidence of Wright and Skinner, His Lordship asked, 'Is that story a deliberate lie, for that is how it is met by the defence, or is it true? There is no halting ground between the two.' While the jury were pondering on these words, he talked about subsequent developments, discussing at some length the testimony of John Guy, and the allegations made in court by Henry Rouse. 'I think the accused must have been extremely unfortunate in the church to which he belongs,' remarked Mr Justice Lawrence. He went on by asking, ' ... do you believe Rouse? If you do not there is only one alternative; Rouse has committed wilful perjury for some reason or another.'

The summing-up continued with a detailed analysis of the handwriting used in the various letters introduced during the trial. The judge paid a singular compliment to Thomas Gurrin, after having first made it clear that he did not generally hold experts in very high esteem. 'I am bound to say that Mr Gurrin is the best of his class; I have known two or three experts who did not give their evidence in the same modest way that Mr Gurrin did.'

Mr Justice Lawrence knowledgeably made sense of the diverse opinions on the letters expressed by the witnesses for both sides, ending his discourse on the correspondence by asking the jury in respect of the letter of assignation, 'The question comes, and a very serious question, too, was that letter written by the accused or not? Upon whoever wrote that letter very strong suspicion is cast, because there is the letter making the midnight appointment; someone kept that appointment; and the result of that appointment was the death of the girl.'

The judge, in reviewing the testimony, compared the balance of probabilities, discarding some theories – 'I do not see how the question of suicide could possibly have arisen, because nothing was found near the girl at all' – while emphasizing other points ... 'there was found upon the accused a knife, and such a knife that might have caused the injuries which were found on the girl'. He expounded upon the knife in detail, particularly with regard to its cleaning and sharpening, expressing the view that 'It is one of those incidents which, by itself, would not be worth a farthing, though with other facts it is more important.'

Before ending, Mr Justice Lawrence briefly mentioned the possible motives for the murder. The public revelation that the murderer had been having an illicit affair with Rose; revenge – for what? – the judge did not make this clear. He even suggested that the crime may have been motiveless, although this seems an unlikely hypothesis.

The jury retired at five o'clock to consider their verdict. Gardiner was taken from the dock and Mr Justice Lawrence retired to his room, while those remaining settled down to await the jury's return.

Over two hours were to elapse before the usher re-entered the court and indicated to the Clerk of Arraigns that the jury were about to return. They filed in to take their places seconds before Mr Justice Lawrence and Gardiner reappeared to take up their respective positions facing each other.

The clerk turned to the jury foreman. 'Are you agreed upon your verdict?' he asked.

'No sir.' There was an immediate murmur in court, quickly silenced as Mr Justice Lawrence said to the foreman, 'You are not agreed? Is there any chance of your agreeing?'

'No sir.'

'None whatever?'

'I am afraid not,' replied the foreman. With that the judge told them, 'I mean if you are satisfied about that, it is my duty to discharge you. You have paid great attention to the case, and the only thing I can do is to make an order that you do not be called upon to serve on a jury again for seven years.'

During the exchange between the judge and jury, Gardiner had made a visible effort to control his feelings, gripping hard the side of the dock. As Mr Justice Lawrence enlarged the bail recognizances of the prosecution witnesses until the next Assizes, he turned as if still dazed by the result, and disappeared from view.

Outside the court the sizeable crowd that had gathered in the rain to await the verdict received the news quietly. They discussed among themselves the justice or otherwise of the result as they saw it, but the question everybody was asking as they dispersed was 'Would Gardiner have to stand trial for a third time?'

Gardiner was to be spared a further ordeal. On Thursday, 29 January 1903, five days after his trial ended, his solicitor, Mr Leighton, received a telegram from the Director of Public Prosecutions notifying him that it was not proposed to put his client on trial again, and authorizing his immediate release from Ipswich prison. Upon receiving the news, Gardiner predictably fell on his knees to give thanks to God for his deliverance.

Gardiner and his family left Peasenhall soon afterwards. It is known that he changed his appearance by shaving off his beard and moustache, but the family's eventual fate is unknown. Rumours abounded – that the couple had opened a shop on the outskirts of London, that they had split up. Another was that Gardiner went to London alone, found a job as a grocer's assistant and was later joined by his wife and children, while again, it was even suggested that they had all emigrated to Canada or North America.

Whatever their fate, it remains a fact that no one else was ever indicted for Rose Harsent's murder. Several of those mentioned in this short account could have had a motive, but it would be invidious now to point a finger at any individual. For all we know Gardiner himself, long since dead, may have taken with him to his grave precise knowledge of what happened on that wild and stormy night in Peasenhall over eighty years ago. If so, those details will remain a secret for evermore.

*Postscript:*

It was said that at Gardiner's first trial the jury were eleven to one in favour of convicting him, while that ratio was exactly reversed when he was tried for the second time. If such was indeed the case and majority verdicts had been acceptable then, as now, Gardiner would not have lived for his second trial.

# 5   A Deadly Rendezvous, Norfolk 1974

Rose Mairne was fifty-two years old, short, plump and bespectacled. A one-time cook at a royal household so it was rumoured, and until her arrest, for six years a housekeeper at a local farm, it stretched one's imagination to visualize her blasting off the back of someone's head with a twelve-bore shotgun. Yet that was precisely what she was accused of as she stood in the dock at Norwich Crown Court in June, 1975.

The story went back to the early hours of Monday, 18 November 1974, when Mairne and her victim, garage proprietor Leonard Thomas Gilford, found themselves together in the pouring rain on the edge of Hockering Wood, some five miles from Dereham.

The circumstances that brought the couple to such an isolated spot have never been discovered. Likewise the conversation that ensued between them was never disclosed. Suffice to say that the meeting ended when Leonard Gilford met a sudden, violent death as the result of a shotgun being discharged a few inches from the back of his head. He was to lie undiscovered where he had fallen for over twelve hours.

A few hours later, twenty miles away at Lingwood, villagers were puzzled when Gilford, a widower who lived on his own in a house on his garage site, failed to open as usual for business. On the previous afternoon he had been chatting and joking with Henry Davison, a friend and neighbour. Nothing had appeared untoward, yet the following morning the garage stayed closed.

Andy Leeder, a mechanic, arrived for work, but finding the premises locked decided to break in. He noticed that the curtains were still drawn in his employer's house, so after a time, with still no sign of Gilford, he fetched a spare key to the house and entered. The scene that met him increased his concern; the normally tidy room looked as though it had been ransacked. Papers were strewn around and an item of women's underwear was on the floor inside the door. The till drawer was out, a bureau drawer was open and loose coins were scattered about. He also discovered that the petrol pump keys were missing. After checking that his employer was not in bed, and after discussing the situation with neighbours, Leeder informed the police. Later that day he and the other villagers were stunned to learn of the popular garage owner's death.

In late 1974, news of Leonard Gilford's violent death in rural Norfolk was overshadowed by two other mysteries of international interest. The disappearance of Lord 'Lucky' Lucan after the murder in Belgravia of the family's nanny, Sandra Rivett, on the night of 7 November, and the disappearance on the 20th of the month of John Stonehouse, the former Labour Postmaster General who vanished into the sea off Miami Beach, to resurface a week later in Melbourne.

An inquest decided in the case of Lord Lucan that he had murdered his children's nanny. It was strongly suspected that she had been mistaken for Lady Lucan. Rumour had it that the relationship between the Earl and his wife had been at a low ebb following reports earlier in the year that their children had been made wards of court, and that divorce proceedings were being contemplated between them. A few days after the murder, Lucan's car was found at Newhaven, and it was assumed that he had fled the country. Despite numerous believed sightings worldwide, Lucan has never been traced, and it is now popularly assumed that he is dead.

John Stonehouse, facing bankruptcy and business ruin, disappeared owing banks and credit companies more than £375,000 and with his companies £300,000 overdrawn. He turned up in Melbourne using an assumed name, but the new life he hoped awaited him with his former secretary was shortlived, as he was detained by the Australian police on Christmas Eve, and in July 1975 he and Sheila Buckley were extradited back to the United Kingdom. Another nine months elapsed before the couple faced trial, but eventually, in August 1976, after a fifteen week hearing, Stonehouse was sentenced to seven years imprisonment for theft and false pretences, while Mrs Buckley received a two year suspended sentence for theft. Stonehouse served a considerable part of his sentence at Blundeston prison near Lowestoft.

*

Leonard Gilford's body was found on the Monday afternoon by Ernest Leonard, a farm foreman who happened also to be a Special Constable. Leonard was driving a tractor past the entrance to Hockering Wood when he noticed a red Austin A40 parked nearby. The vehicle was still there when he returned later, so he stopped to investigate. On the other side of the gate to the wood, lying on a concrete path, Leonard saw the body of Gilford, quite obviously dead. Wasting no time, Leonard hurried off to inform the police.

The first detective to arrive at the scene was Constable Brian Gare. He immediately made a search of the area and found, lying on the ground near the body, a cartridge case and a small piece of paper on which was written a solicitor's name and telephone number. There were also signs of shot on nearby trees, but no trace of a weapon.

Sixty-five-year-old Leonard Gilford was a friendly, hardworking man. An excellent mechanic, with many friends, he nevertheless retained his independence and rarely discussed his private life. He was also a man of regular habits, and so it was that on Sunday, 17 November 1974, he followed his usual routine by driving into Norwich to have dinner at Boswells, one of his favourite restaurants. As he was leaving he made a curious reply when asked by his waiter if he was going on to make his customary visit to his regular public house, the Bell at Salhouse. 'No,' he replied, 'I am going out to the woods.' The waiter, who half thought Gilford was joking, asked him, 'What, Thetford?' to which the other responded,

'That way. I am meeting someone and they are taking me there.' Nevertheless, Leonard Gilford did after all first go to the Bell, leaving there later never to be seen alive again.

Lodge Farm, Rollesby, was the home of octogenarian Geoffrey Rose and two of his three sons, Harold and Maurice. In 1969 Rose Mairne had taken up the post as housekeeper to the three men. During the next six years the affable, hardworking woman was employed at the farm, often helping out on the land when not working indoors. Both the Rose sons later spoke highly of her, describing her as 'a marvel about the house' and 'a first-class cook'. More recently she had involved herself in the finances of the farm, not a wise move as both her own funds and those of the farm were in a parlous state. The bailiff was a frequent visitor, while she herself was in debt to several people. By November 1974 it seems that Mairne, if not her employer, was facing a financial crisis.

Whilst Gilford was enjoying his pint in the Bell at Salhouse, on that wet Sunday evening Mairne had driven Mr Rose senior to the Lodge public house at North Tuddenham, nearly twenty miles away. It was originally intended that they should meet Mr Rose's third son Peter and his wife for a drink, but Mairne had earlier contacted Peter and cancelled the arrangement, explaining that she had to go to Swanton Morley on business.

After depositing her employer at the Lodge and buying him a drink, Mairne departed after telling the landlord that she was going to Swanton Morley and would be back later to collect Mr Rose. She returned just after 11 p.m. as the pub was closing. It was noticed that she arrived from the opposite direction to that from Swanton Morley. She explained her lengthy absence by telling a customer that her car had had a puncture, a statement later disproved. Mairne and Geoffrey Rose drove back to the farm, where soon after the old man went to bed. Some time later Mairne went out again into the miserable November night, her destination Hockering Wood and a meeting with Leonard Gilford.

It was not immediately apparent to the investigating officers whether the death of Leonard Gilford was a case of murder, accident or suicide. After Detective Constable Gare had left the scene, the whole area was cordoned off and uniformed police officers were drafted in to widen the search he had made for the weapon and other clues. Their lack of success predisposed Detective Chief Superintendent Reginald Lester, head of Norfolk CID, and his team in the major incident room at the Divisional Police Headquarters, Dereham, to the conclusion that they were investigating a murder rather than the alternatives.

In the meantime another detective, Sergeant George Wallace, had gone back to Gilford's house at Lingwood after visiting the scene. Nothing had been interfered with since Andy Leeder, the mechanic, had entered earlier. Wallace was soon in no doubt that someone other than Gilford or Leeder had been into the house and left it in its disordered state. The next day he returned, and after a closer search he found a wall safe concealed behind the pantry door, which when opened was found to contain £502 in cash.

The first indication that Rose Mairne may have known something about the events at Hockering Wood came with the interviewing of the solicitor whose name and telephone number was on the piece of paper found at the scene. The information he supplied prompted the investigating officers into making closer enquiries about the housekeeper at Lodge Farm.

As a preliminary step, Detective Sergeant Keith Young visited the farm two days after the murder. After being greeted by Mairne, he told her that he was enquiring into the death of Leonard Gilford. Mairne explained that on two occasions she had spoken to Gilford at his garage about changing her car, but after learning of his death from the television she had not even realized that it was the same man. After some further discussion Young produced the piece of paper found at the scene. Mairne studied it and then said, 'That's the note I gave to the poor old man ... I gave it to him so that he could ring my solicitor, who handles my financial affairs.'

She enlarged on this later in a written statement, explaining that during the course of a business meeting with her solicitor, he had written his name and telephone number on the piece of paper which she had later given to Gilford with instructions that if he found her a suitable car, he was to contact the solicitor.

Prior to Detective Sergeant Young's visit on Tuesday, Mairne had seen the two Rose sons and Ronald Munford, a county court bailiff who was familiar with the financial situation at Lodge Farm, depart for London. The arrangements had been made following a telephone call from Mairne to the bailiff explaining that it was necessary for the two sons to travel to London with him to sign some papers concerning a will; there they were to book into a hotel and await her arrival the following day. However, after the unwelcome visit by Sergeant Young, Mairne altered her plans and never left for London, leaving the perplexed trio to return to Norfolk with their mission unaccomplished. Harold and Maurice Rose arrived back to find Lodge Farm deserted. Unnerved by Sergeant Young's visit, their housekeeper had left the day before, taking their father with her.

The sudden departure of Rose Mairne and her employer from Lodge Farm immediately strengthened police suspicions. Enquiries were intensified, and it was not long before there was enough evidence to warrant her later being charged with obtaining over £1,000 by deception, in addition to any more serious charge.

Mairne's powers of persuasion were remarkable. £25 borrowed from a female relative of her employer, on the understanding that she had been left a legacy that she could not immediately draw upon. Peter Rose, the third Rose brother, had lent her £30. She 'phoned him on 20 November and asked for a further loan which, he said, she needed to send to his brothers in London. This time she was unlucky, for Peter refused to help her. So it continued; an obliging antique dealer at Acle, a Martham shopkeeper, and over £1,000 from a haulage contractor at Blofield, none of whom had been repaid. A possible motive for Gilford's murder was emerging.

Her temerity, born probably out of necessity, did not stop after she and her employer had hurriedly left the farm on 19 November. She telephoned two acquaintances and persuaded the first to send her over £160, and the second a further £60. A third man later testified that he agreed to pay for the repairs to her hire car. During the next four weeks Mairne and the elderly Mr Rose travelled round the south east of England. From Brancaster on the north Norfolk coast, through Melton Mowbray, Datchet and Windsor, to Fetcham in Surrey's stockbroker belt, where she was finally arrested.

On the evening of 20 November, the couple called at the home of a friend at Melton Mowbray, where Mairne made several telephone calls, offering as payment some cigarettes she had in her car. One whom she contacted was an acquaintance from whom she had already borrowed considerable sums of money, and who again responded to her request by posting off to her a further sum of money the next day. Mairne later telephoned her benefactor's home and confirmed with his wife that the money had been dispatched. What Mairne's future plans were are not known, but by December her travels around the country were nearing their end.

Both Harold and Maurice Rose had been subjected to long, intensive police interrogation a few days after the murder, but both had subsequently been released. It was Harold, in fact, who later handed to Detective Constable Gare a shotgun that he owned. The weapon, a twelve-bore, single-barrelled shotgun, was examined by a ballistics expert who, after microscopically comparing a test cartridge fired from it with the cartridge case found at the scene of the murder, stated unequivocally that it was the murder weapon.

With the motive, means and opportunity established, together with a mass of circumstantial evidence, and her sudden departure from Lodge Farm, Detective Chief Superintendent Lester decided that when traced, Mairne should be brought back at once to Norfolk for questioning.

Her arrest at Fetcham in Surrey was soon to follow, and on 10 December 1974 Lester and Rose Helen Mairne had their first introduction at Great Yarmouth police station. The subsequent questioning of Mairne continued for three days with her consistently, and often vociferously denying having shot Gilford. She also mentioned the bizarre events that she said had led up to his death, and which were to be elaborated upon at her trial. While Mairne was being interviewed, her hire car was searched. In the boot were found two more shotgun cartridges and three keys, later found to fit the petrol pumps at Gilford's garage. Finally, three days after her arrest, Rose Helen Mairne was charged with Gilford's murder; five other charges were also preferred alleging that she had obtained by deception a total of £1070.

Mairne's first appearance before the Great Yarmouth magistrates was on 13 December 1974. Four months were to pass before committal proceedings started on 22 April 1975. These culminated after two-and-a-half days with her committal in custody to later stand trial at Norwich Crown Court.

Before she stood in the dock at Norwich on 16 June 1975, Mairne had been further charged with entering Leonard Gilford's house and stealing ladies underwear, cigarettes and some keys. The deception offences, to which she pleaded not guilty, were not proceeded with on the directions of the judge.

Mr Felix Waley, QC, the Crown counsel, after telling the ten men and two women of the jury in his opening address that the circumstantial evidence was overwhelming, went on to describe Mairne as 'a cold-blooded killer with an apparent motive of greed that was satisfied in the end only to the extent of a few cigarettes and some second-hand underclothes'.

He alleged that Mairne and Leonard Gilford had met near Hockering Wood. 'We shall never know the nature of that appointment,' he said, 'but its result was that Mairne shot dead Mr Gilford, took the key to his conservatory from his pocket and went to his house where she believed a large amount of money was kept. Mairne was in debt and needed money ... ' Unfortunately for her Gilford kept only a little cash in the concealed wall safe; she had to content herself with some of the late Mrs Gilford's underclothing, a quantity of cigarettes and keys to the garage petrol pumps. Her chagrin can be imagined, as she realized that she had horribly miscalculated and had slain Gilford for so insignificant a reward.

Mr Waley then briefly outlined the events leading up to Gilford's death, and the police investigation that followed. During her interrogation by the police, he said, Mairne had alleged that Gilford had been involved in lorry hijackings, the smuggling of currency abroad, the disposal of stolen goods and other 'villainy' as she termed it. She had claimed throughout that Gilford's death was an accident, saying the gun had gone off after he had tripped over in some undergrowth. Mr Waley admitted that the fatal injury to Gilford could have been self-inflicted, although he said this was unlikely due to the heavy trigger pressure necessary to fire the weapon.

It was during the police questioning, he went on, that Mairne had first referred to a third party called 'Timmy', who she said had been present at the shooting and had run away with the shotgun after the 'accident' had occurred. Finally, before calling his witnesses, Mr Waley described the events following Gilford's death, with particular reference to the people Mairne had contacted requesting money.

The Crown counsel's opening speech, a fine example of an advocate's oratorical skill, befitted one who later became a circuit judge, and left the jury with a clear picture of the case that the prosecution intended to prove.

On the second day of the trial Professor Geoffrey Gresham, a Home Office pathologist, testified as to the cause of death; he said that it was likely that the gun had been discharged between one and two feet behind Gilford's head, and estimated death as having taken place between midnight and 2 a.m. Professor Gresham conceded that the wound could have been self-inflicted, but expressed doubt as to this having happened. 'All I can say is that having seen many suicidal shotgun wounds, I have only seen one suicidal wound that ever looked anything like this ... To have been self-inflicted, it would have to have been pointblank.'

After Ernest Leonard had told of finding the body, and Detective Constable Gare had given evidence of attending first the murder scene and later Lodge Farm, where he had taken possession of Harold Rose's shotgun, Detective Inspector Richard Bass, a fingerprint expert, gave encouragement to the defence by stating that despite having thoroughly checked Leonard Gilford's house for fingerprints, none belonging to Mairne had been found.

During the next two days a succession of witnesses attested as to the normality of Gilford's movements and behaviour during the days immediately preceding his death. Evidence was also given by three experts from the forensic laboratory at Nottingham. The first was a Mr Norman Lee, a principal scientific officer. Although a prosecution witness, he gave added comfort to the defence when he stated that examination of various exhibits in the case failed to establish a link between the defendant and Leonard Gilford. He went on to say that examination of the stomach contents, in conjunction with the known time of his last meal, led him to expect Gilford to have been dead by midnight. This differed from the opinions of Geoffrey Simpson, a fellow scientist at Nottingham laboratory, and of Professor Gresham, both of whom estimated death as having occurred some time after midnight.

As has so often been the case in murders by shooting, the most decisive witness for the Crown was the ballistics expert. Thomas Alfred Warlow, also from the forensic laboratory at Nottingham, had compared the cartridge case found at the scene of the murder with test cartridges fired from the shotgun later retrieved from Lodge Farm. 'There is absolutely no doubt in my mind that this cartridge was fired from this weapon,' was Mr Warlow's unshakeable conclusion. He continued, ' ... my findings indicated a raking shot aimed at the right of the deceased's head, from back to front, and fired from very short range.' There was another crumb of comfort for the defence when Warlow said that in his opinion it was possible that the wound was self-inflicted, although it would be rather unusual.

Other witnesses during Wednesday and Thursday included Ronald Munford, the county court bailiff, and Derek Ellis, a police mechanic. Munford, who had been persuaded by Mairne to accompany Harold and Maurice Rose to London, said that on a number of previous occasions when he had called at Lodge Farm with county court orders he had always been met at the door by Mairne, while Ellis disproved her statement that her car had sustained a puncture on the evening of 17 November.

After listening during the morning of the fifth day to a number of witnesses from whom Mairne had borrowed money during 1974, the judge, counsel and jury were taken from the court first to the Lodge public house at North Tuddenham, and then on to the murder location. There the party remained for nearly half-an-hour, enabling everyone to visualize more clearly some of the events that were being described in court.

The final prosecution witnesses were heard on Monday, 23 June, the start of the trial's second week. The day was devoted to the police testimony; the officers' evidence, given in the unemotional, matter-of-fact manner typical of police witnesses, introduced more drama into the trial.

Detective Chief Superintendent Reginald Lester had led the

investigative team, and had had lengthy interviews with Mairne after her arrest. He told the court that when he had first suggested to her that she had killed Gilford and then entered his home to search for money, Mairne's violent response had been to bang on the table with her fists and shout at him, 'Come off it sir. I am a liar, a thief and a cheat, but I have never used violence to anyone.' She continued to deny having either known or killed Gilford, or having had anything at all to do with his death.

This all changed at a subsequent interview with Mr Lester. For reasons known only to herself she adopted a diametrically opposite stance. Instead of denying all knowledge of the events surrounding Gilford's death, she had introduced a third party, 'Timmy', and admitted that she had been present when Gilford died; when pressed as to who had killed him she repeated, 'I can't tell you. I can't; I can't.'

Later she further admitted having known Gilford, and said that she had earlier lied about this to protect herself. In reply to Mr Lester's question, 'What happened that night?' Mairne had replied after some hesitation, 'Timmy gave me the key out of his pocket and told me to go to the house and take all the things I could find and take them to him at Hunstanton. I was not there when he was shot.'

Mairne's confusion was apparent as later when asked again who had shot Leonard Gilford, she had said, 'No one, it was an accident. The gun just went off. I took the gun there and brought it back, but I didn't shoot him.' Mr Lester had pressed her, 'Why rob him?' to which she had replied, 'You have no idea what I went in that house for or why Lenny went to the woods.' Asked if she had entered Gilford's house to search for money, she had said 'I am not saying.' With that the policeman had had to be content.

The questioning had been continued by Detective Inspector Roy Hipperson and Detective Constable Clifford Holmes. In the witness box Hipperson said that Mairne had told him, 'It was an accident, a pure accident. I didn't think anyone could make it murder … he killed himself. He fell over something in the undergrowth. He always took the gun when we met him there.' When questioned again on why she had gone to Hockering Wood at that time of night, she had replied dramatically, 'Villainy was going on. They were getting money out of the country. It was a very big fiddle … The money I got was always new. A lot of foreign money came into the country.'

Yet again she had been quizzed on what had transpired at the wood, allegedly replying, 'According to Timmy a couple of sounds were heard and he fell in the undergrowth. He turned him over, grabbed the gun and bolted.' Later Mairne was guilty of further inconsistency when she told Detective Inspector Hipperson that she had herself taken the gun back to the farm.

She had referred again to the 'shady deals', alleging that notes were sent abroad in the exhaust systems of cars on which Gilford had worked. She had enlarged on this when questioned by Detective Constable Holmes. She told him first, 'That terrible man has charged me with murder. He has ruined my life or what is left of it. But I shall go into court with dignity.' When asked by Holmes if she had received money from Gilford she had indignantly replied 'Not a penny', adding that they were mixed up in 'other things ... I did it for money, but I think Lenny only did it for kicks, because he had been bored since his wife's death.'

The following day Mairne's interview with Holmes had continued. She had told him, 'We used to meet in the country to dispose of stuff from lorries ... Mostly I dealt with Timmy from Hunstanton, but we never used surnames.' Her final remark to the detective was both a denial and an admission, 'Murder is ridiculous. It was an accident. I know because I was there.' To Detective Chief Inspector Geoffrey Neville, the last policeman to interview her, she had admitted, 'I am a villain but not one who takes somebody's life. The two just don't go together.' Throughout her questioning by different detectives, she had consistently, frequently with some vehemence, denied that Gilford had been deliberately shot. Mairne showed little emotion as the police officers followed each other into the witness box to testify. Occasionally she blinked, owl-like behind her spectacles, as her alleged replies were related, but otherwise she sat placidly with her hands folded in her lap.

The first surprise when the defence opened its case on the seventh day of the trial was the announcement by Mr John Marriage QC, Mairne's counsel, that he would not be calling upon his client to testify. 'She will not be giving evidence,' said Mr Marriage, 'as she has already been under the tremendous strain of being accused of such a serious crime. That strain and stress is even greater when you are a person who has been stigmatized and attacked by the prosecution as a congenital liar.' Mr Marriage told the jury that he would be calling evidence 'which, you may think, casts an enormous amount of doubt on the suggestion that Mrs Mairne committed murder.'

One of his first witnesses was Harold Rose. Mr Marriage introduced Rose by telling the jury that he had been a suspect at one stage and had been interrogated by the police. Whether this was a judicious admission to make is arguable. Rose told the court that his father and the accused had gone out together about 6.30 on the evening of the murder. He later went to bed, but heard them return between 11.30 and 11.45 p.m. This coincided with the time that the police earlier had contended the murder had taken place, and therefore alibied Mairne. However, it will be remembered that two out of three forensic experts had placed Gilford's death as having occurred between midnight and 2 a.m., which would have allowed Mairne ample time to travel from Rollesby to Hockering, meet Gilford and return to the farm by morning.

When giving evidence and during cross-examination, Harold Rose made no attempt to conceal his animosity towards the police. He agreed that his earlier statements had been misleading. 'Do you honestly think you are going to get the truth when a man jumps over the table at you and says you're mental? Do you honestly think you're going to help the police? ... I was bitter,' he admitted.

Later there followed each other into the witness box three people each of whom said they had noticed a second vehicle, if not at the scene, at least in the vicinity.

Mr David Grey told the court that as he cycled to work past Hockering Wood at 7.30 a.m. on Monday, 18 November, he had noticed a red A40 and a blue mini-van with the back open on 'the wood side of the gate'. Under cross-examination Grey insisted that it was on the Monday morning that he had noticed the blue van.

Another witness, farmer Albert Wales, caused some confusion in the minds of those present by stating that he had not noticed any vehicle parked in the entrance to the wood as he drove past at 2.15 p.m. on the Monday, but upon returning a short time later an empty red car was parked outside the gate. He said that earlier the same day he had been passed in Stone Road by a blue van containing a single occupant, being driven towards the wood.

A third reference to both an A40 and a blue van was made by Mrs Janet Jackson, who stated that on several occasions during 1974 she had seen an A40 and a blue Ford Escort in Stone Road. She had noticed two men, both in their fifties, sitting in one car or the other.

An expectant murmur went round the court as the name Geoffrey Rose was called, and all eyes were on the old man as he entered the courtroom and made his careful way round to the witness box. After explaining that Mairne had been in his employ for six years, he went on to describe the events of Sunday evening, 17 November, as he remembered them. He said that when Mairne arrived back at the Lodge public house after having left him there earlier, they both returned to the farm, arriving there at about a quarter-to-midnight to find Harold waiting up for them. Harold it will be remembered, had earlier testified that he had been in bed and had been awakened by their return.

The witness continued by saying that about fifteen minutes after returning to the farm, Doris, as he called Mairne, had gone out leaving him and his son in the kitchen. He said that within half-an-hour she returned and did not go out again that night.

Under cross-examination Mr Rose denied knowing anything of his housekeeper's financial problems. He agreed with Mr Waley that in a statement made to the police, he had said that when he went to bed his housekeeper was still downstairs, and the next he remembered was his son Harold bringing him up a cup of tea in bed.

When the time arrived for opposing counsel to make their closing speeches, both referred to the statements Mairne had made. Mr Waley dismissed her utterances as those of 'a congenital liar', whose 'greed for money – and need for money, might well be the motive', while Mr Marriage sought to persuade the jury that despite the Crown's insistence that it was 'moonshine', there was 'a great deal of evidence to suggest that there was villainy, or at least something going on involving other people.'

Whilst admitting that no one would ever know what induced Leonard Gilford to go to Hockering Wood, or for what purpose, Mr Waley poured scorn on Mairne's assertions that together with herself and other shadowy people, he had been involved in unlawful activities, principally relating to the illegal exportation of currency. 'The Crown suggests that it is the romancing of someone trying to find an excuse,' he declared. He maintained that the truth lay nearer to the statements Mairne had made to the police. She had told one officer that he would find a lot of money in Gilford's house, while to another she had remarked, 'He was supposed to have a lot of money hidden in the house.'

Mr Waley dismissed the possibility of either suicide or accident, pointing out that 'there was nothing to suggest an accident except remarks by the accused, upon which no reliance could be placed at all.' After referring to the 'fantasy world in which the prosecution say this penniless woman lived', Mr Waley spoke of the conservatory key, 'A vital factor in the prosecution case was the conservatory key found in the kitchen drawer at Lodge Farm. It would mean that the key must have been in Hockering Wood in the early morning of 18 November, and that Mr Gilford's pockets were rifled to obtain that key.' Undoubtedly the key found in Mairne's kitchen drawer was one of the most difficult and incriminating pieces of evidence with which the defence had to contend.

Mr Marriage in turn conceded that his client's reputation for truthfulness – probably rightly – had been blackened and besmirched, ' ... But I ask you to bear in mind what she did not say [to the police], because what she did not say was "I did it" '. He contended that although the Crown had dismissed her 'villainy' allegations as 'moonshine', there was evidence to suggest that at least there may have been an element of truth in what Mairne had said. With the uncertainty that surrounded certain aspects of the case there was a real danger of a wrong verdict being returned, he said.

Mairne's counsel advanced three possible theories as to why Leonard Gilford had gone to Hockering Wood on that wet November night. That he went alone, followed by Mairne with the shotgun; that she lured him there; or that he went to meet one or more other people. Mr Marriage dismissed the first two alternatives as being at best unlikely. He favoured the third option as being worthy of serious consideration, 'You may think the only explanation is that he was going there to meet some other people,' he suggested to the jury.

Mr Marriage reminded the jury of David Grey's testimony as to having seen a blue mini-van as well as the red A40 as he was on his way to work on the Monday morning. 'Can you possibly dismiss David Grey?' counsel asked, 'Why should the van be there? One possibility which they might think remote was that it was there to remove the body ... You may think that the theory, however far-fetched it may seem at first blush, is one that is at least worth considering.' He pointed out that there were 'great patches of doubt – these areas of mystery', indicating that the prosecution case was riddled with doubt.

Mr Marriage circumvented the evidence pertaining to the conservatory key by pointing out that after examining a hundred items, seventy belonging to Mairne, the forensic scientists had found not a single link between her and Gilford, a point that he said should register in her favour. It is interesting to speculate on the jury's view of this information when weighed against the indisputable fact that the conservatory key had been found in the accused woman's kitchen drawer.

After advising them that it would be unsafe to infer that the intruder who entered Gilford's home was also his killer, he told the jury that Mairne's defence rested on the alibi that she was at Lodge Farm at the time Leonard Gilford met his death.

Mr Marriage sat down after finally reminding the jury of two comments his client had made to the police. The first had referred to her own character shortcomings; the second explained that Gilford's death had been an accident. No one would later dispute Mr Justice Willis's epithet when he described as 'brilliant' John Marriage's defence of Rose Helen Mairne.

Before the jury retired to consider their verdict on the eleventh day of the trial, they heard Mr Justice Willis say that it was a 'troublesome, difficult and anxious case'. He told them furthermore that it was a very remarkable case, and he urged them to reject speculation when deciding the issue and to 'stick to the evidence'. He said that although the jury may think that clearly the motive was to obtain money from Gilford, it was not incumbent on the prosecution to prove that. He pointed out that Mairne's decision to refrain from giving evidence under oath was her right, but added that it might have been helpful to the jury if she had gone into the witness box to explain some of the circumstantial evidence that had been tendered.

The judge reminded the jury that the defence contended that with so many gaps and areas of doubt, the prosecution had failed to prove its case. In any event he said, if the alibi defence was accepted by the jury, that would be an end to the matter. If on the other hand the jury believed the alibi to have been concocted, it was obviously valueless.

While East Anglians had been absorbed in the Mairne trial, elsewhere other events had occupied people's attention. The trade unions, for instance, were expressing their disquiet over the Labour government's policy of wage restraint, being unilaterally opposed to a statutory incomes policy.

On a happier note, as the Mairne jury were considering their verdict, Billie-Jean King, at thirty-two, was on the way to her sixth Wimbledon final, beating twenty-one-year-old Chrissie Evert 2-6, 6-2, 6-3 in the semi-final. It was an unhappy week for Chrissie, as two days later it was reported that she and the men's champion, Jimmy Connors, had scrapped their wedding plans.

James Robertson Justice, the actor, died in his sleep at his home near Winchester on the day that the verdict was announced, while on a more quixotic note Raymond Fletcher, Labour MP for Ilkeston, promised a national meeting of French prostitutes that he would raise their problems with French colleagues in the Council of Europe.

Back in Norwich after the jury had retired, Mr Justice Willis had gone to his room and Mairne had been returned to her cell, the court assumed the air of false normality that superimposes itself above the tension that exists during a jury's absence. Counsel, who only a short time before had been in total opposition, chatted amiably, one with another. Police officers spoke together, discussing anything but the outcome of the case, and witnesses who had remained in court after testifying sat self-consciously, wearing the slightly bemused expression common to those unfamiliar with the procedures in a criminal court.

Five hours had passed by the time the jury re-entered the court and filed back into their box. After Mr Justice Willis and Rose Mairne had resumed their places, the jury foreman, in answer to the court clerk's question, announced that they had unanimously found the prisoner guilty both of Leonard Gilford's murder and of entering his home and stealing various items of property.

Mairne slumped to the floor of the dock as the verdict was announced, and as court officials and prison officers hastened forward to help her, it is doubtful if she heard Mr Justice Willis as he sentenced her to life imprisonment.

The Crown against Rose Helen Mairne was an extraordinary case. As Mr Justice Willis remarked to the jury, 'There are matters which you may think will remain mysteries to the end of the case, and maybe to the end of time.' Among other riddles, he was probably referring to the reason for Leonard Gilford's fatal trip to Hockering Wood. Mr Marriage had advanced three possible theories to explain the victim's nocturnal drive. It may be interesting to briefly look again at this baffling aspect of the case.

Why should a man of excellent local repute, hardworking and of regular habits, drive twenty miles on a wet November night to rendezvous at a lonely wood with a person who within a short time of his arrival would blast him into eternity? One must disregard Judge Willis's adjuration to the jury, and speculate. A romantic assignation? This was not even mentioned by Mr Marriage as the possibility was too remote, and there was no evidence whatsoever to suggest such a link between the couple. A financial transaction? Possibly; although not a rich man, Leonard Gilford was comfortably off, and would certainly not have been the first person to have been induced by Mairne to part with money to help resolve her financial problems. But why should such a transaction take place at such a time and place? Privacy could have been ensured elsewhere.

Mention should be made of Mairne's defence submission that she and Gilford were both involved in illegal activities involving third parties, one of whom, 'Timmy from Hunstanton', was also present when Gilford accidentally shot himself. The jury rejected this explanation after having had the benefit of listening to all the evidence, so it would be invidious now to resurrect it as a serious proposition. However it is reasonable to point out that by dismissing this explanation the jury also rejected the evidence given by David Grey, Albert Wales and Mrs Janet Jackson as to the presence of a blue van, variously described as a mini-van or a Ford Escort, at or near Hockering Wood on the day Gilford was found and before.

Were all three witnesses mistaken as to what they had seen, or the day on which they had seen it, or had they drawn a false conclusion from their sightings? If none of these, the question that begs an answer is, what was that second vehicle doing at or near the scene – was there a connection?

There remains the explanation that Mairne lured Gilford to Hockering Wood with the express intention of shooting him, then taking the keys of his house which she later entered to search for the ready cash that she believed was there. This was the solution put forward by the prosecution at the trial, and accepted by the jury. In the absence of a feasible alternative it seems the most likely explanation.

Another intriguing question asks where did Mairne go to earlier on the evening of Sunday, 17 November 1974, after leaving her employer in the Lodge public house? If, as she said, she had gone to Swanton Morley on business, what was the nature of that business at that time on a Sunday evening? If Swanton Morley was not her destination, where did she go, and what kept her away for over two hours? It is another question among several that remained unanswered.

Finally, Rose Mairne herself. Greedy, dishonest and scheming she would admit to being, but throughout her questioning and trial she strenuously denied being the heartless and cold-blooded killer of Leonard Gilford. Described variously by those who had known her as good-humoured, lively and keen-minded, it is difficult to reconcile her affability with the callousness she must have displayed on that November night in 1974. She was, and remains an enigma.

# 6  Murder at Moat Farm, Essex 1899

Occasionally a character emerges who for good or evil has a charismatic effect upon those with whom he comes into contact. Such a person was Samuel Herbert Dougal. A big man over six feet tall and sixteen stone, with a neatly trimmed beard and an air of worldliness born of his twenty-one years in the army, his appeal to many women was irresistible. In turn he was attracted not only by their comeliness, but by a healthy bank account.

At the time he met Camille Holland, Dougal was fifty-two years old and married to his third wife, the first two having died in highly suspicious circumstances whilst he was serving in the army. After leaving the Royal Engineers in 1887 with the rank of Quartermaster-Sergeant, he took various jobs until after two years he sailed for Dublin where he met and married Sarah White in 1892.

For the next three years he divided his time between England and Ireland until in 1895 he started work as a hospital messenger in Dublin. It was soon after he had been dismissed for dishonesty, that he was convicted in England of theft and forgery and sentenced to twelve months hard labour. Shortly after arriving at Pentonville prison he made an abortive attempt to hang himself. As a result he was committed to an asylum where he served out the remainder of his sentence.

Despite this unfortunate episode, his predatory appetite for women remained; his marriage and the arrival of three children did nothing to dampen his ardour. A succession of mainly wealthy females succumbed to the blandishments of the burly, well-dressed and rugged-looking ex-soldier, only to find later that there was another brutal side to his nature from which they were quick to flee.

Sarah White stayed longer than most, but a few months later even she found his behaviour unbearable, so she returned to

Dublin. This suited Dougal, as it left him unhindered in his pursuit of other agreeable women. It was during this period that he was to meet Camille Holland, an encounter that for both of them was to end in tragedy and death.

Camille Cecile Holland epitomized the classic Victorian spinster. A petite woman of fifty-five, fastidious about her appearance, she was not unattractive. Born in India, she had been brought up by an aunt in England. A genteel, devout Catholic, Camille experienced a tragic love-affair when young, since when she had settled down to a life of spinsterhood. In 1893 her aunt died leaving her a legacy amounting to about £6000, some stocks and shares and various items of jewellery. The income she derived from the investments enabled the retiring, middle-aged lady to enjoy some of the pleasures she earlier had foregone, but which her newly acquired wealth and status now allowed.

She chose to stay in hotels and boarding-houses, writing occasionally to her nephews, her nearest relatives. There is nothing to suggest that Miss Holland was anything other than an ageingly attractive, modest Victorian lady of independent means, until that is, she had the misfortune to meet Samuel Herbert Dougal.

The couple first met either at the Earls Court exhibition or as the result of an advertisement in the columns of a matrimonial paper. Whatever the true circumstances of their introduction in September, 1898, Miss Holland was staying at the Bayswater boarding-house of Mrs Florence Pollock when she was visited by Captain Dougal as he called himself.

It was an opportune time for Dougal to appear on the scene. Soldiers and ex-soldiers alike were soon to be revered when news of Kitchener's Anglo-Egyptian army's defeat of the Khalifa's Dervishes at the Battle of Omdurman reached home. Reports of the charge of the 21st Lancers, 'which cut a path of blood for itself through the Dervish masses', raised the stock of the Victorian soldiery to unprecedented heights. Dougal was not slow to take advantage of the situation; although he had left the army eleven years before, he quickly realized that the simple expedient of calling himself Captain would likely endear him to susceptible females.

Camille soon became enamoured of her military-looking suitor, and within a month had agreed to stay with him for a weekend at the Royal Hotel in Southend.

Dougal truly believed that he had struck gold. Miss Holland had imprudently misled him into thinking that she was better off than was in fact the case, and now his sole aim was to gain control of her wealth. However he was over-zealous, for in November, only two months after they had first met, he tried to persuade her to withdraw all her money for him to invest in his name. Although infatuated, Miss Holland was still astute enough to see through Dougal's machinations, so she abruptly ended their affair.

Dougal realized that he had blundered but, determined to retrieve the situation, he called again on Miss Holland, who soon succumbed once more to his blandishments. Soon afterwards the couple moved from London into a rented house at Hassocks, near Brighton, paid for of course by Miss Holland.

Dougal did not enjoy their time together in Sussex. 'I did not find Miss Holland as generous as I expected,' he said later. 'We went about a great deal, and most of the expenses were paid by me. I didn't have very much money, but what I did have I soon got through, and that was why I suggested we should buy a farm.'

That was only partly true; Dougal was certainly short of money, but he had also decided that the time had arrived for him to settle down to a more leisurely existence. He planned that Miss Holland should buy a farm and transfer it to his name. He in turn would sell it and live comfortably off the proceeds.

After viewing several properties, Dougal eventually entered into negotiations to buy Coldhams Farm near Clavering in Essex. Miss Holland again gave evidence of her business acumen during these transactions by travelling to London and having the contract entered into by Dougal ostensibly on her behalf, substituted by one naming herself as the purchaser. A fortnight later, preparatory to moving into the renamed Moat Farm, the couple left Sussex to lodge at an address at Saffron Walden, only a few miles from their future home. They remained there for three months during which time Mrs Wiskin, the landlady, and Miss Holland became friendly as a result of their mutual affection for 'Jacko', Miss Holland's little brown and white dog. It was to Mrs Wiskin that Camille confided some of her reservations about Dougal; nevertheless by the time she moved with him to Moat Farm on 27 April 1899, the landlady had decided that they were an affectionate and devoted couple.

Dougal had chosen well in the farm for what by now he had in mind. Set deep in the Essex countryside, it was isolated, surrounded by trees and had no close neighbours. Its most unusual feature was a moat which completely surrounded the property, and which was spanned by a single narrow bridge to give access to the house. A smaller moat to one side was fed by a drainage ditch which crossed the farmyard. As Dougal said later, 'It was just the place I wanted, and I thought the moat would be very useful, because after the farm had been transferred to me I thought it might be easy for the lady to be found in the moat ...'

A couple of days after their arrival at Moat Farm, Dougal and Miss Holland were joined by a servant girl, Lydia Faithful, who, however, was soon replaced by nineteen-year-old Florence Havies. Dougal, scenting another conquest, surprised Florence early on the first morning after her arrival by creeping up behind her in the kitchen and kissing her. To his disappointment Florence's reaction was not what he had hoped for. Instead of responding, she objected strongly and complained to Camille, who had difficulty in persuading the girl to remain.

Two nights later Dougal, undeterred, tried to enter Florence's bedroom. She screamed for Miss Holland, who arrived on the scene as she fainted. This time Florence was determined to leave the farm at the earliest opportunity, but again she was prevailed upon by a distressed Camille to stay.

After spending two nights sleeping with Miss Holland in the spare bedroom to avoid Dougal's unwelcome attentions, the end of an unhappy week for Florence came on Friday, 19 May. During the evening her mistress came into the kitchen to tell her that Dougal and herself were going out. Soon afterwards, with a cheery, 'Goodbye Florrie, I shan't be long' from Camille, the couple departed in the pony and trap. It was the last time that anyone apart from Dougal is known to have seen Camille Holland alive.

For Dougal the time had arrived; he had decided since being at the farm that the only sure way to gain control of Camille's money was to dispose of her permanently. He discarded schemes involving drowning or accidental shooting, in view of the consequent inquest and likely enquiry by her relatives. Eventually he decided that the most convenient way would be to shoot Miss Holland and conceal her body in the farm's drainage ditch, which on his instructions was already being filled-in by local labourers.

After leaving the farm on the Friday evening, the couple drove into Stansted before returning home at about a quarter-past-eight. It was a balmy spring evening and Camille lingered before going indoors, remarking to Dougal on it being a beautiful, moonlit night.

Dougal later recalled his version of the shooting:

> 'I had pushed the trap into the coach house by this time, and I could see by the light at the back of the house that the servant girl was still there doing her work. I stepped up on the side of the trap, reached down for the revolver [previously hidden in the barn], and as Miss Holland stood just near the door looking at the moon I shot her. I wasn't standing very far from her, and of course I was a little higher, because I was still on the step of the trap. She dropped like a log, and then I pulled her into the coach house.'

For the rest of the night Dougal was occupied with the disposal of the body. He interrupted his labours on five occasions to return to the farmhouse; the first time to tell Florence, to her consternation, that her mistress had suddenly gone to London, and later to explain that she had not been on the trains that he said he had been to meet. Florence spent the night apprehensively sitting fully-dressed by her bedroom window. Dougal meanwhile fortified himself with brandy before contemplating various ways of ridding himself of the body. Finally he returned to his original plan of burying it in the drainage ditch.

Having made up his mind he lost no time in completing his gruesome task. When he had finished he went to bed, but not surprisingly, despite the brandy he had consumed, sleep eluded him, so he got up and for the remainder of the night prowled around the farm.

He said afterwards, 'I am sure I aged that night twenty years. I never closed my eyes the whole night long, and I could not keep still or rest for even a quarter of an hour. I tried to write, tried to sleep, but it was all in vain. Not one single moment's peace did I have, and I am sure that if I went once to the ditch I went twenty times.'

All the while Dougal was in the farmyard that night, Florrie Havies was sitting by her bedroom window, oblivious of the nightmarish activity being carried out only a few yards away.

With the daylight Dougal recovered his composure. He told Florence Havies that he had received a letter from Miss Holland that morning saying that she was 'going to have a little holiday'. It is doubtful if Florrie was very interested, as in response to her summons her mother was due to arrive that morning to take her home. Mrs Havies duly arrived and departed soon afterwards with her daughter, leaving Dougal to contemplate one of the labourers filling in the drainage ditch, a task that was completed within a few days.

He was not to remain alone at the farm for long; soon after the servant girl had left, he summoned his wife and daughter who had returned from Ireland and had been staying in a nearby village. He had earlier explained to his wife that Miss Holland was financing his purchase of the farm, and that soon she would be leaving on a health cruise. With the arrival of his wife and daughter he felt able to relax, and to concentrate on the immediate task of gaining access to, and control of, his former beloved's money and assets.

All went according to plan; to his few neighbours he explained his wife's presence by introducing her as his daughter. In time even that pretence was abandoned, with Mrs Dougal revealing to the vicar's wife, Mrs Frances Morton, her true identity. Surprisingly the revelation excited little comment.

When satisfied that his forging of Miss Holland's signature would deceive her bankers and stockbrokers, Dougal began regularly to draw upon her assets. Cash withdrawals, the sale of her holdings and the settlement and transfer into his name of Moat Farm provided him with the wherewithal to slip easily into the role of a benevolent country landowner. His generosity – he subscribed towards a clock for Clavering church – helped ensure that he was soon accepted into the rural community. For almost four years Dougal was to enjoy the fruit of his labours on that May night in 1899.

He had never intended that the farm should be a thriving, profit making concern, but rather a quiet retreat where he could enjoy his amoral pleasures undisturbed. He would therefore have been largely unaffected by the agricultural depression that reached its zenith at the turn of the century. His servant girls, mainly recruited from neighbouring landworkers' families, were paid on average a mere £15 per annum, for which they were expected to be on call day or night. Nonetheless, dependent as many families were on the daughter's contribution to the family budget, when many of the girls discovered that for such a paltry wage they were expected to acquiesce to Dougal's unwelcome overtures, they had no hesitation in packing their bags and leaving. It was of little consequence to Dougal; servants were plentiful, and the occasional girl was always prepared to co-operate.

When Queen Victoria died in January, 1901, Dougal was at the height of his fraudulent prosperity. One can easily imagine him, the prestigious landowner, travelling to London in his newly acquired motor car, one of the first to be seen in the locality, to pay his loyal respects to the monarch whom he had served for over twenty-one years.

Admittedly there were rumours of strange happenings at his farm; for instance it was said that the owner derived considerable entertainment from watching buxom country wenches peddling bicycles furiously across his fields. A mere eccentricity of the wealthy the locals at first thought, until one evening a farm worker told his disbelieving companions that earlier he had suddenly been confronted by the young women who to his astonishment were in a state of complete undress.

As the months passed a succession of younger, more nubile, albeit impoverished young women passed through Moat Farm; many, arriving alone, left sadder, if not wiser, with the prospect of another mouth to feed in a few months time. Not surprisingly Mrs Dougal was unhappy at the situation, and quarrels between them became frequent, culminating in her leaving the farm in January 1902 in the company of a labourer named Killick.

Dougal sought solace in the arms of Kate Cranwell, an eighteen-year-old servant girl who had arrived a month prior to his wife's departure. It was Kate who was to lead to Dougal's exposure. In September 1902 she left the farm as she was pregnant, to be immediately replaced by another girl who within two months found herself in a similar condition.

The 'goings on' at Moat Farm were now the talk of the countryside. Dougal was drinking heavily, and at one Bacchanalian orgy he reputedly seduced three daughters and their mother. To make matters worse Kate Cranwell, who had commenced affiliation proceedings, and his estranged wife, voiced aloud the misgivings of many regarding Miss Holland's disappearance four years earlier. It was inevitable that sooner or later these openly expressed suspicions should reach the ears of the local constable, PC James Drew, who wrote a letter to his Chief Constable: ' ... it is now said that it was Miss Holland's money that bought Moat House Farm and people think he must have done away with her and buried her.' Although Dougal was unaware of it, PC Drew's letter signalled that the 'good life' was coming to an end.

The letter, dated 30 January 1903, led to immediate enquiries being instigated; it was soon established that Miss Holland's bankers, stockbrokers and solicitors had all been deluded into believing that they had been communicating with her for the past four years; even the local postmistress had seen their letters arriving for Miss Holland. Superintendent Charles Pryke of the Essex Constabulary was deputed to visit Dougal and question him informally regarding the rumours circulating in Clavering, particularly those relating to Miss Holland's disappearance.

Dougal disclaimed all knowledge of Camille's whereabouts, 'I know nothing about her and have not seen her since I left her at Stansted railway station about three years ago,' he said. 'She left nothing belonging to her behind in my house ... We had a tiff a few days before she left in consequence of my servant, a girl of about eighteen years of age, telling her that during the night I tried to enter her bedroom, which was false ... If she had any money or any railway shares or stocks, I was not aware of it.' His convincing manner satisfied Pryke, who said later in the witness box, 'I thought he had told me the truth, and I shook hands with him on leaving.' Pryke was to revise this opinion when a few days later, after speaking to Detective Inspector Alfred Mardon, a warrant was issued for Dougal's arrest on a charge of forgery.

Dougal, despite his apparent confidence, had taken fright at Superintendent Pryke's visit, and had withdrawn a total of over £600 from two bank accounts; nine days later he left the farm. It is inconceivable that by now he was unaware that the net was drawing tighter, but despite this he was determined to have a last fling. So on Friday, 13 March, he stayed overnight in London, and on the next day met by arrangement the pregnant servant girl who had succeeded Kate Cranwell. They travelled to Bournemouth where they spent a long weekend together at the Coburg Hotel. The following Tuesday the girl returned to the farm, while Dougal remained in London.

The next day he walked into the Bank of England and asked William Lawrence, the cashier, to change some of the £10 notes that he had withdrawn from his bank two weeks before. Lawrence recognized the notes as some that had been stopped, so he summoned Detective Inspector Henry Cox of the City of London police, who was on duty at the bank. Dougal refused to account for the nine £10 notes he had presented, so Cox told him that he would have to accompany him to the detectives' office at Old Jewry for further questioning. On the way Dougal tried to run off, but he was soon caught and overpowered.

Later at Cloak Lane police station he was charged by Inspector Mardon with forging Camille Holland's name to a cheque the previous August and obtaining the sum of £28.15.0d.(£28.75). Asked if he understood the charge, Dougal replied, 'Yes, that is quite right; I understand perfectly well what you mean.'

Two days later on Thursday, 19 March, he appeared before the magistrates at Saffron Walden charged with the cheque forgery.

During the five remand hearings spread over the next six weeks, the magistrates were subjected to a mass of evidence concerning Miss Holland's financial affairs, and the many and varied transactions allegedly carried out by Dougal since her disappearance. A succession of witnesses testified as to letters received purportedly written by Camille Holland, and to countless cheques and other documents bearing what was believed to have been her signature.

Meanwhile the police searched Moat Farm and uncovered a considerable amount of property and clothing identified as having belonged to the missing woman. The unlikelihood of her having left the farm leaving this behind encouraged speculation that she was perhaps nearer to hand than Dougal would have them believe. After determining that she was not concealed in any of the farm buildings, the searchers turned their attention to the land immediately surrounding the farm.

For several weeks a team of policemen systematically dug up the farmyard. Often working waist-deep in slime, they persevered day after day, uncovering everything but that which they sought. Someone then suggested that if the labourers who had been working at the farm four years before could be found, they may be able to narrow the search. So it proved; Henry Pilgrim was traced and indicated the line of the former drainage ditch.

Conditions here were even worse for the seekers after Miss Holland, with sewerage and liquid manure instead of mud. However, their single-mindedness was about to be rewarded. On the afternoon of Monday, 27 April, almost six weeks after they had started, a constable forked out a lady's button boot containing the remains of a foot; also exposed through the filth was a piece of

dress material. Further careful excavation revealed what remained
of Camille Holland. A contemporary newspaper report describing
the state of the remains said that 'A brief examination showed that
the body, which was lying face downwards, was in a crumbling
condition, the foot having broken off with the boot when the latter
was pulled up. Otherwise the body was intact.'

Events moved swiftly after the body's discovery. Mrs Henrietta
Wiskin, the landlady at Saffron Walden, identified some of the
clothing that was on the remains, and an inquest was opened two
days later in the large barn that dominated the farmyard. The
proceedings which took place on three separate days, with a
week's adjournment between each, ran concurrently, with the
police court hearing of the forgery charge, resulting in some of the
witnesses appearing in both courts.

Mrs Florence Bakewell, née Havies, relived some of the events
that had taken place four years before. 'Mr Dougal put his arm
around my waist and kissed me, at which I was much annoyed,'
she said. She went on to describe his efforts to enter her room two
nights later ... 'there came a knocking, and Mr Dougal called
"Florence" in an undertone. I knew his voice. He called "Florence"
three times in an undertone. I asked him what he wanted. He was
pulling my door as hard as possible, and I screamed for Mrs
Dougal. He nearly wrenched the bolt off.'

Mr Pearce, the Treasury Solicitor, asked the former servant girl
about Miss Holland's departure on the evening of 19 May 1899.
'Did you see her go?'

'Yes, from the front door. The prisoner was with her. I saw them
drive away in the pony and trap.'

'Did you see any luggage?' asked Mr Pearce.

'No she had no luggage,' Florence replied.

'Was anything said by Miss Holland or the prisoner when they
drove away?', next asked Mr Pearce.

'No; only Miss Holland when she went out of the door, said,
"Goodbye Florrie, I shall not be long." '

'Did you ever see her again?'

'No.' Finally,

'Were you expecting her back that evening?'

'Yes.'

Dr Augustus Joseph Pepper, of St Mary's Hospital, London,
was another who testified in both courts. He had carried out the
post-mortem on the remains of Miss Holland at the farm. He

described how, 'On the right side of the skull, above and behind
the ear there was a round aperture ... on the left side of the head
there was a more or less circular aperture.' Dr Pepper had
discovered a bullet inside the skull and explained that 'The bullet
entered on the right side and was arrested on the left, after driving
out the bone on the left side. The bullet wounds could not have
been self-inflicted. The position of the wound indicated that the
shot had been fired from behind. The direction taken by the bullet
was from above, down forwards and to the left ...'

The Coroner, Mr C.E. Lewis, on the last day of the inquest,
recapitulated on the circumstances leading up to Miss Holland's
disappearance, the discovery and identification of her remains and
the cause of her death. He finally enjoined the jury that, 'If satisfied
with the evidence, I think I might safely say that it is your duty to
return a verdict of wilful murder against Dougal.' The jury agreed,
and after giving their verdict listened as Dougal announced,
'Gentlemen, I am a perfectly innocent man.'

Meanwhile, on Thursday, 30 April, the opening day of the
inquest, Detective Inspector Marden had visited Moat Farm
where, in the dining room, he had charged Dougal with Miss
Holland's murder. Henceforth evidence was to be heard relevant to
the murder as well as to the forgery allegations.

On 6 May 1903, at Saffron Walden police court, Dougal was
formally charged with the murder, after which Detective Sergeant
Scott gave evidence of finding the body, Mrs Wiskin of identifying
it and Dr Pepper of the post-mortem. Mr Arthur Newton,
Dougal's solicitor, referred Mrs Wiskin back to the evidence she
had given at the inquest. 'Do you not agree that the articles you
identify as belonging to Miss Holland are of the most ordinary
kind, which could be bought in numbers of shops?'

'Yes.'

'And they have no name or mark to enable you positively to
identify them?'

'That is so.' Mr Newton continued,

'Before the Coroner did you say, "I recognize the features?" '

'Yes.'

'What did you mean by swearing you recognized the features
when they do not exist?'

'Because I could recognize the head and teeth and the small feet.'

Dr Pepper confirmed that the teeth were remarkably
well-formed. He estimated the age of the deceased woman as

between forty and sixty, and said that in his opinion she had been
dead between three and five years. Under cross-examination he
dismissed the possibility of suicide.

At subsequent hearings Kate Cranwell, the servant girl seduced
by Dougal at the farm, told the court that she had seen a revolver
there; George Mold, a bootmaker, positively identified as his work
the boots disinterred with the remains of Miss Holland, and
Thomas Gurrin, a handwriting expert, testified to the spuriousness
of documents which since 1899 had purportedly been written or
signed by Miss Holland.

At last, on Friday, 29 May 1903, just over four years after Miss
Holland had died, Dougal, still protesting his innocence, was
committed to stand his trial at the next Assizes sitting at
Chelmsford.

The crowd assembled outside the Shire Hall at Chelmsford on the
morning of Monday, 22 June 1903, were hoping to gain
admittance to a trial that they anticipated would last for several
days. Only a handful eventually got in, to be disappointed when
the trial ended after only two days.

During the three weeks since his committal, Dougal had proved
to be a prolific correspondent. His wife, daughter, friends and
ex-lady loves were among those to whom he had written. Probably
the most bizarre letter was the one he wrote to one of his former
girlfriends inviting her and others to his trial: 'I daresay the girls
have received their notices, etc., to attend next Monday at
Chelmsford, have they not?' he asked. 'There will be several from
about there, and it would be a good idea to club together and hire a
trap and drive all the way. It is a delightful drive through
undulating country, and at this time of year it would be a veritable
treat for them all. So much better and more comfortable than the
train ... ' It is not known how many of the young ladies partook of
the suggested excursion.

Those in court listened as Mr Charles Gill, the Crown counsel
who two years before had successfully prosecuted Herbert
Bennett, the Yarmouth murderer, opened the Crown case. In his
quiet, imperturbable manner, Gill outlined the circumstances
surrounding the first meeting between Dougal and Miss Holland,
their subsequent journeyings together and the events following
their move to Moat Farm. He suggested that the murder had been

committed before the couple had returned to the farm on the evening of 19 May 1899, and that Dougal had then taken the body back and deposited it in the drainage ditch, a version that differed from that of Dougal himself.

Mr Gill went on to describe briefly events that had taken place subsequent to Camille Holland's disappearance. The arrival at the farm of the prisoner's wife; the numerous business transactions he had conducted with Miss Holland's unsuspecting banker and stockbroker and the police enquiries, including the interview between Dougal and Superintendent Pryke. In his relatively short opening address, Mr Gill laid to rest the hypothesis and rumour that had been circulating since the police had started investigating Camille Holland's disappearance.

As he called his witnesses the seriousness of the proceedings was lightened when Mrs Florence Pollock, Miss Holland's former landlady, identified a juryman as the man who had twice visited Camille when she was staying at her address. 'Will you kindly remove your veil, madam?' requested Mr Gill courteously.

'Yes, oh yes, now I can see him,' repeated Mrs Pollock, pointing again at the embarrassed member of the jury. With the spectators chuckling, Mr Gill patiently tried again, 'Will you kindly listen to me for a moment, madam? Look slowly round the court again.'

'Yes, there is the gentleman.' A dozen pairs of eyes swivelled round to settle this time on the Shire Hall keeper whom Mrs Pollock was now indicating.

Mr George Elliott, Dougal's counsel, impishly intervened to point out that, 'This lady has identified a gentleman on the other side of the court.' Mr Gill persisted, repeating slowly and deliberately, 'Will you do what I ask, madam, and look around the court slowly please?' This time, much to his relief, the witness pointed to Dougal, 'That is the man sitting there.' At last the amusement, in which Dougal had wholeheartedly joined, subsided.

For the third time in as many months, Florence Bakewell recounted the sequence of events that had taken place during her week at Moat Farm in 1899. After she had repeated her earlier testimony, Mr Elliott, in his cross-examination, tried to establish that a generally harmonious relationship had existed between Dougal and Miss Holland. 'Did the prisoner and Miss Holland appear to be on friendly terms?' he asked.

'Yes, so far as I could see,' replied Florence.

'If there was any trouble between the prisoner and Miss Holland, then it arose out of him kissing you?'

'I don't know about that.'

'There was no other trouble that you were aware of?'

'Not that I was aware of.'

After questioning her about Dougal's general behaviour whilst she had been at the farm, Mr Elliott concluded by asking Florence if she had returned to Moat Farm since leaving with her mother. 'No, I was glad enough to get away,' she replied feelingly.

The invidious position in which Superintendent Pryke had found himself during his interview with Dougal was plain to see as he testified. He had been instructed to have an informal chat with Dougal in an effort to resolve the rumours circulating locally about Miss Holland's disappearance. Consequently he had neither cautioned Dougal, nor informed him that what he said may be used against him.

Mr Elliott's objection to the Superintendent's evidence being admitted, was overruled. As much of what Dougal had told Pryke was proved to be false, and undermined his case, his counsel's objection is understandable. Pryke frankly described the interview, but the lack of explicit instructions resulted in much of his evidence in turn being undervalued.

Detective Sergeant Scott, after telling again of the finding and identification of the body, revealed that, 'On 4 May I found in the Moat Farm a box of thirty-four revolver cartridges loaded; they were in a tin in a shut-up cupboard in the kitchen. They were covered with seed, and could not be seen until the seed was removed.'

Later, Henry John Churchill, a gun, rifle and ammunition manufacturer with thirty-five years experience, told the court how he compared the bullet found in Miss Holland's skull with bullets extracted from the cartridges found by Detective Sergeant Scott. His conclusion was that ' ... it is similar to the others, the same size and calibre.' Mr Churchill's rudimentary comparison made visually and by weight, preceded by several years the introduction of Goddard's Comparison Microscope, which brought a far more sophisticated technique to bear on the subject. (See Chapter 11).

Kate Cranwell, the eighteen-year-old servant girl made pregnant and subsequently discarded by Dougal, testified that sometime after June 1902 he had given her two gold rings, and that later she packed a trunk with women's clothing that appeared to belong to

Miss Holland, which she thought had then been sent to Mrs Dougal. She went on to say that whilst at the farm she had seen Dougal throw three letters addressed to Miss Holland into the fire after first reading them, she had also seen 'some firearms, some guns and a revolver; I saw the revolver in August last, and I saw some cartridges.' As Kate stepped down from the witness box, Dougal surely regretted for once in his life his indiscretions with a servant girl.

Other prosecution witnesses testified as to the devious methods adopted by Dougal in pursuing financial and business transactions since he had met Camille Holland in 1898, and which established beyond question that greed was his overriding motive in killing her. When the final witness for the prosecution had been heard, there remained only the closing speeches of counsel and the summing-up of Mr Justice Wright. Despite the suggestion that there were young women still sufficiently enamoured of him to speak in his defence, Dougal had opted not to call any witnesses. He also declined to go into the witness box himself, being content to rely upon the eloquence of his counsel to save him from the gallows.

Mr Gill's closing speech to the jury after lunch was short, a lengthy exhortation rendered unnecessary by the overwhelming evidence against Dougal.

The Crown submitted that it had conclusively established both that the remains found in the ditch were those of Miss Holland, and that she had been murdered. Mr Gill then moved on to the motive, the opportunity and the identity of the culprit. Dougal's continuing residence at the farm, he said, depended on Miss Holland's benificence and his continuing appeal to her; the latter he had seriously jeopardized by his indiscreet and unwelcome advances towards Florence Havies, as she was then. Camille had been distressed all the week following his behaviour, and as Mr Gill pointed out to the jury, 'if she took any steps in consequence of his conduct he would revert to his original position of being a man without means.'

We have already seen that Dougal had ample opportunity; living in an isolated farmhouse with no close neighbours, having only Camille and a servant girl for company, and with a drainage ditch in the yard already half filled-in, he had chosen well for the deed he had in mind.

Mr Gill ended by referring to the manner in which Miss

Holland's affairs had been conducted since her death. It was only after Superintendent Pryke's visit almost four years after her disappearance that Dougal had lost his nerve by trying to dispose of the farm, attempting to draw as much ready cash as possible from his bank accounts besides taking with him small, easily negotiable items of jewellery when he fled the farm. 'The cumulative facts,' said Mr Gill, 'are consistent only with the guilt of the prisoner.'

A daunting task faced George Elliott as he rose to make his speech on Dougal's behalf, aware as he was that on his eloquence and no less depended his client's life. He did his best, but the case against Dougal, although entirely circumstantial, was prodigious. As in the Bennett case, when Edward Marshall Hall had attacked the press for its unprofessional behaviour, so did Elliott open his peroration to the jury by claiming that an attempt had been made 'to try him [Dougal], by a tribunal other than this', and that some of the arguments and inferences drawn 'have not been all of the fair, judicial nature'. He then sought to undermine the Crown case by suggesting that Mr Gill had presented a 'terribly suspicious case', but one nevertheless that was devoid of absolute proof.

He emphasized the problems attached to the identification of a body in an advanced stage of decomposition, drawing attention to the discrepancies that he said existed between the height, age and build of Miss Holland before and after death. Mr Elliott scored a useful point by drawing attention to the absence of any identifying marks on the clothing found on the remains, whereas all Miss Holland's clothing discovered at the farm was so marked. He dismissed as unreliable the evidence of Mrs Wiskin, who had identified some of the clothing, but he was not so easily able to dispose of the testimony of George Mold the bootmaker, who had positively identified the boots found on Miss Holland's feet as his work. The best Dougal's counsel could do was to suggest that boots other than Miss Holland's could have been made on the same lasts for someone else years before.

Moving on to whether Dougal was Miss Holland's killer, Mr Elliott questioned the feasibility of killing a woman who provided Dougal with financial and emotional security. By killing her he would destroy the source of both. He underplayed Dougal's dalliance with Florence Havies, 'the little incident in regard to the servant', as he put it. Camille's response to that 'little incident' may well have precipitated her death.

Before ending, Mr Elliott made a second telling point. 'You are asked to believe,' he said to the jury, 'that the prisoner brought the body back to a spot which was visible from the bedroom window of the house.' This was the window at which Florrie Havies was supposed to have sat all night. Mr Elliott said that it was inconceivable that Dougal would have disposed of Miss Holland's body in the drainage ditch in view of the servant girl.

Before sitting down Mr Elliott referred briefly to Miss Holland's furniture left at the farm – a guilty man would surely have disposed of it. He closed with an appeal to the jury that 'Through me as a last appeal, the prisoner trusts that the jury will be able to say that the case has not been proved against him ...'

There remained only the summing-up; Mr Justice Wright's charge to the jury embraced briefly and succinctly all the salient points made by both sides. He opened by paying tribute to the 'fairness, courage and skill' of the prosecutor, and to Mr Elliott's 'eloquent speech.' After warning the jury that 'more than usual care is required' in considering a case where the evidence is entirely circumstantial, he moved to the question of identity; after referring specifically to the evidence of Mrs Wiskin and the bootmaker George Mold, the judge asked, 'If it was not the body of Miss Holland, whose body was it?' He then mentioned the fact that Dougal was the last person to have been seen with Miss Holland on the evening she disappeared, remarking that, 'There is certainly a grave case against the prisoner.'

While giving due weight to the point made by Mr Elliott regarding the improbability of Dougal disposing of Miss Holland's body within view of the bedroom window, Mr Justice Wright reminded the jury that, 'in the darkness of night the task of disposing of that body would not be a difficult one'.

The judge mentioned also the furniture belonging to Miss Holland that remained in the house after her death. It was entitled to the jury's consideration he said, but added significantly, 'The prisoner seems to have been very careless by leaving all sorts of traces of Miss Holland about the place.'

After commenting on Dougal's lack of concern after Miss Holland had disappeared, 'when one would have expected that the whole country would have been disturbed', Mr Justice Wright ended with a reference to the 'very powerful motive in this matter ... the lady's fortune ... There is no doubt at all that the prisoner got her fortune into his hands'.

The jury were out for exactly an hour-and-a-quarter considering their verdict. When they returned to announce that they had found the prisoner guilty, Dougal remained impassive, and made no reply when asked if he had anything to say before sentence of death was passed. After being sentenced he turned smartly in the dock and disappeared from view.

Dougal's appeal was predictably dismissed. He then petitioned the Home Secretary with no greater success. This was not surprising in view of the catalogue of lies his petition contained; in a last desperate effort to save his neck, he now confessed to shooting Miss Holland, but said that the revolver had 'accidentally exploded'. After having solicitously enquired 'I hope you are not hurt dear', he said that he had given her some brandy and then carried her into a field hoping that either the breeze or the brandy, or perhaps a combination of both, would revive her. Neither remedy worked and Miss Holland expired. Not knowing then what to do, he wrote, he finally decided after first kissing her and decorously placing a piece of lace over her face, to bury his loved one in the farm's drainage ditch.

This amazing document, amounting to several hundred words, and written in the third person, besides meticulously recording the dates of the police court and inquest hearings, included the full name of the trial judge, 'the Honourable Sir Robert Samuel Wright', and the counsel who appeared for both sides.

Considerable time and effort must have been expended by Dougal's legal advisors on compiling the petition; acting as they were on his instructions, and aware that it was his last forlorn hope, it would nonetheless be surprising if they were unaware of the futility of their efforts and the likelihood that the contents would more probably increase the prejudice against their client than excite the sympathy of the man to whom it was addressed.

Dougal was executed at 8 a.m. on Tuesday, 14 July 1903. He went to his death bravely, as befitted a former soldier of the Queen. As he stood, white-capped and pinioned, waiting for the trap doors to fall, the chaplain, the Reverend Blakemore, twice asked him, 'Dougal, are you guilty or not guilty?' After the second time Dougal replied, 'Guilty' as the trap crashed open.

So on a sunny morning in July ended the life of a scoundrel who in the most calculated and cold-blooded manner had in his turn ended prematurely the life of a lady who craved nothing but a little happiness and affection. In return she was prepared to offer devotion and material assets in the hope that these would ensure their future happiness and prosperity.

Miss Holland's tragic misfortune was to meet a man who would not hesitate to go to any length, or adopt any measure that would satisfy his insatiable desire for physical and material self-gratification. He ruined the lives of countless young women who met him either accidentally or by design. The Victorians, many of whom were themselves guilty of covert immorality, frequently invoked double standards, offering little comfort or sanctuary to an unmarried girl with an infant.

Dougal did not concern himself with such problems. When he had tired of his current favourite, or she had discovered to her dismay that she was expecting a child, it was futile appealing to him for financial or other help. He rid himself of them as speedily as possible and then sought a willing replacement.

Miss Holland offered him the opportunity of fulfilling his material need. If she had been prepared to surrender her wealth unconditionally to Dougal, there is the faint possibility that she would have survived. Her presence on the scene would have provided the cloak of respectability which he coveted. Miss Holland however, realized early on that Dougal was almost exclusively preoccupied with her material assets. This awareness effectively sealed her fate. She had been on her guard since his premature and clumsy attempt to secure control of her wealth in November, 1899, but a simple understanding of her lover's avarice and intent was not enough, and she was pathetically ill-equipped emotionally and intuitively to handle the devious, scheming individual with whom she was convinced she was in love.

After killing Camille, Dougal's subsequent behaviour virtually guaranteed that he would ultimately be detected. The surprising thing was that he remained at liberty for almost four years. During that time while deceiving astute professional men with his forgeries, he was simultaneously leading a life of debauchery at Moat Farm without arousing suspicion or comment until the last few months.

When he was eventually exposed, the investigation, inquest and trial were completed with a rapidity that tempts one into speculating on whether the authorities were anxious to get the whole sorry affair over with as soon as possible, in the hope of minimizing the publicity and embarrassment of those concerned. If such was the intention, it failed dismally. The Moat Farm

Murder has passed into the annals of crime, to be written and talked about by succeeding generations.

# 7   Death of a Landlady, Cambridgeshire 1964

Domenico Borzillo was worried. It was two days since he, or any of his three fellow lodgers at the house in Emery Street, Cambridge, had seen or spoken to Cacilie Wollner, their fifty-eight-year-old Swiss-born landlady. Domenico was sure that she would have mentioned it had she decided to go away for a few days, but nothing had been said. He wondered if perhaps she was ill and unable to summon help? There was only one way to find out; he went downstairs and knocked on the door to her room. There was no answer or any sound of movement from within. Uncertain as to what to do next, he went outside and round to his landlady's bedroom window through which he peered. As a result of what he saw he hurried back indoors, told the others and then telephoned the police. A woman's half naked body was lying on the bed with what appeared to be an eiderdown covering her top half.

Detective Chief Inspector Joe Breed of Cambridge CID was puzzled and not entirely satisfied about the death of Cacilie Wollner. A post-mortem carried out by Dr Geoffrey Gresham, a university pathologist, had not gone beyond confirming that death was not due to natural causes.

Suicide appeared the most likely explanation. For eighteen months prior to December 1963 the dead woman had been a patient in Fulbourne Psychiatric Hospital in Cambridge, and since leaving there she had occasionally received electrical treatment at the out-patients department at Addenbrooke's Hospital. Despite this, the suicide theory did not tie in with the injuries sustained by Cacilie Wollner before her death. The empty cash box found in her bedroom also worried Breed. Admittedly a similar box found nearby still contained £1.10s. (£1.50), and almost £400 had been found elsewhere in her room, but it was certainly not unheard of for a thief to panic for some reason, leaving money or valuables behind.

The discovery of a middle-aged woman's dead body in somewhat unusual circumstances excited little attention in Cambridge or elsewhere during the summer of 1964. Abroad the United States was in its third year of involvement in the Vietnam war. At home, while politicians were preparing for a general election, people were elated at news that Donald Campbell had exceeded 400 m.p.h. in breaking the world land-speed record in far-off Australia. On a grimmer note, in West London police were investigating the fifth similar murder of young women in eight months.

Rhys Llewelyn Hopkins was tired, dispirited and very worried. Sitting in the car he had stolen four days previously in Middlesbrough, the twenty-one-year-old hotel worker thought back over the past four weeks and pondered on what next to do.

His present troubles had started with the break-in at his former lodgings at Emery Street a month ago. Not realizing that his ex-landlady was in bed as he climbed through her window, he had panicked when she had woken up. He couldn't remember exactly what happened after that, apart from returning to his lodgings in Windsor Road, seeing blood on his raincoat and noticing that his feet and trousers were soaking wet.

The next day he had set off for his home town of Middlesbrough. There was nothing much there for him apart from unhappy childhood memories, so he had left after a few days and returned to Cambridge in a car that he had taken. There he soon learnt that Cacilie Wollner was dead. He suspected then that he would be in deep trouble if the police caught up with him, so again he left Cambridge, this time to head south.

Now he was stranded in Essex without petrol in a stolen car. Suddenly Hopkins was brought back to the present by a policeman opening the door to ask what he was doing. He explained that the car had run out of petrol and that he intended returning to Cambridge, at the same time getting out as though to go for petrol. He had no sooner returned empty-handed, than the policeman reappeared. This time his questioning was more persistent. Suddenly it was all too much for Hopkins, 'I'm fed up', he blurted out, 'Can I talk to you?'

News that a man had been arrested in Essex and had made a statement admitting the Emery Street burglary a month previously, galvanized Joe Breed and his colleagues. It was Wednesday, 12 August 1964, four weeks to the day since Cacilie

Wollner had died. No time was wasted in having Hopkins conveyed back to Cambridge where Breed, Detective Inspector F.C. Lilley and several others were awaiting him. It was Lilley who questioned Hopkins first. After informing him that he was enquiring into the break-in at Miss Wollner's house, the detective asked, 'What room did you go into?'

'Miss Wollner's room,' Hopkins replied.

'Was the landlady there?'

'She might have been out,' answered Hopkins uncertainly.

'What, at 3 a.m.?' said Lilley.

'She might have been in another room.'

The questioning was continued by Detective Chief Inspector Breed who, after telling Hopkins in his turn that he was enquiring into Cacilie Wollner's death, asked him where she was as he entered her room. Hopkins replied that she had been in bed, but he couldn't remember if she had called out or if he had thrown an eiderdown over her. Breed asked him if he had been holding anything when he had broken in, to which Hopkins replied, 'I may have had a chisel in my hand,' proffering the additional information that, 'the window was open a little way at the top. I didn't have to force it. I levered it up from the bottom with the chisel.' He admitted to having been on edge and said that he may have lost his temper when in the room. Upon returning to his lodgings he had been, 'sweating all over and shaking', and had noticed the blood on his clothing as he was getting ready for bed.

As the questioning continued, Hopkins told Breed that he was unable to remember if he had taken any money from Miss Wollner's bedroom, and when pressed as to what had in fact taken place that night, he said, 'I do not know whether I hit her or not.' Eventually he agreed to make a written statement admitting that he had gone out with the intention of breaking in somewhere, and had taken with him a torch and chisel for the purpose. He described how he had entered Miss Wollner's room and had seen the cash boxes and banknotes, and how after hearing a movement from her bed he had lost his temper. After that he could not remember anything until he had arrived back at his lodgings, exhausted and sweating. He ended his statement by describing his subsequent movements until he was arrested.

Although Breed and Lilley had enough to charge Hopkins with the break-in and car theft, for which he was to appear in the magistrates court the next morning, they needed more conclusive evidence as to the cause of death to go with the statement before it would be safe to charge him with capital murder. It was therefore decided to have the body exhumed and re-examined.

Meanwhile a chisel and raincoat recovered from Hopkins, along with a sample of Cacilie Wollner's blood, and the pillow from her bed, were forwarded to the Metropolitan Police Laboratory for forensic examination.

Cacilie Wollner's body was disinterred during the early hours of 8 September and taken to Addenbrooke's Hospital where Dr Francis Camps, the Home Office pathologist, was waiting to carry out a second post-mortem. The police were hoping that this would throw more light on the cause of Cacilie's death, but they were to be disappointed. Camp's findings largely coincided with those of Dr Gresham's examination carried out seven weeks previously. Camps later testified that none of the injuries he found was severe enough to have caused death, going on to agree with Geoffrey Gresham that although asphyxia played a part in Cacilie Wollner's death, everything pointed to her having died from shock.

Breed now had the results of two post-mortems, neither of which was particularly helpful so far as a murder prosecution was concerned, a written statement from Hopkins admitting that he had broken into Cacilie Wollner's bedroom, but recalling little else, and the results of the laboratory tests. It had been impossible to group the blood found on the chisel, but that on Hopkins' raincoat was found to be of group 'B', the same as Miss Wollner's. Hopkins' blood was of group 'O'.

Was that enough to justify charging him with capital murder? Apparently the Director of Public Prosecutions thought so, for on Friday, 18 September 1964, Rhys Llewelyn Hopkins appeared again before Cambridge Magistrates, further charged with having killed Cacilie Wollner in the course or furtherance of theft.

The committal proceedings eventually lasted for three days. Hopkins, sitting composed in the dock, listened as Mr Hugh Cossham outlined the prosecution case. The discovery of Miss Wollner's body, her face ' ... extremely red and suffused', was followed by details of Hopkins' arrest and interrogation by the police. Mr Cossham admitted that the cuts found on Miss Wollner's body did not cause her death, ' ... death was due to asphyxia or shock ... the prosecution will prove that she died as a result of what Hopkins did that night'.

After evidence had been given of the body's discovery and

identification, Drs Gresham and Camps told the court the results of the respective post-mortems they had carried out on the body. The doctors agreed as much on what did not cause death, as to what had. Finally, Detective Chief Inspector Breed and Detective Inspector Lilley described Hopkins' arrest, his subsequent questioning and the written statement he had made. All the while Hopkins listened, showing little emotion as the prosecution case continued.

Between the committal on 21 September, and the opening day of the trial on 11 November, Hopkins' solicitors worked hard on preparing his defence. They had already contacted two consultant psychiatrists who had treated him as far back as 1955, and now arranged for a consultant psychiatrist in forensic psychiatry to examine him whilst he was on remand in Brixton prison. Finally the principal medical officer at the prison was to be called by the defence. Hopkins was certainly to have a formidable array of medical expertise speaking on his behalf.

6d. (2½p) on income tax and the same amount on petrol thereby increasing the price of a gallon to 5/8d. (28p), were the main topics of conversation late on Wednesday, 11 November 1964. The contents of James Callaghan's emergency budget introduced that afternoon, only a month after a Labour Government had been elected, completely overshadowed the opening day of a trial whereby a twenty-one-year-old hotel worker stood charged with capital murder.

Dense fog that had shrouded the whole of Eastern England during the night had lifted sufficiently to allow the trial's main participants to arrive safely in time for the ten o'clock start. The trial, much of which would consist of medical evidence, was presided over by Mr Justice Thesiger. Mr P. O'Connor had the responsibility of defending Hopkins, while the Crown case was in the hands of Mr E.D. Sutcliffe. Hopkins' solicitors and Mr O'Connor agreed that he would not be called to the witness box and that his only witnesses would be the psychiatric and medical experts who would testify as to his state of mind.

The trial opened with Mr Sutcliffe introducing the prosecution case. He alleged that Cacilie Wollner had died as a result of asphyxia and shock, directly attributable to Hopkins, who had broken into her house and departed taking with him a sum of money. Under the Homicide Act, 1957, this act made him liable to the death penalty.

Dr Geoffrey Gresham, describing the post-mortem he had carried out, told the court of cuts he had found on the body, agreeing with counsel that it was 'quite possible' they could have been inflicted with a chisel, but adding that it was unlikely that they could have caused death. He went on to say that the purple discolouration of Miss Wollner's face could have resulted from lack of oxygen, following partial suffocation, this in turn inducing the shock leading to her death. The doctor agreed under cross-examination that some of the wounds could have been self-inflicted, an indication perhaps that Mr O'Connor was not relying entirely on a defence of diminished responsibility.

Dr Francis Camps agreed with his colleague. In his view the wounds to Miss Wollner's hands had come about as she tried to fend off her attacker shortly before she died. Of the other wounds to the upper part of her body, Dr Camps said, 'I could not conceive that these wounds were inflicted with the intent to cause any serious injury. They are the sort of wounds inflicted deliberately to cause pain or fear.' He added that suffocation had definitely contributed to Cacilie Wollner's death.

While a thirty-three-year-old man was being sentenced to life imprisonment at Oxford Assizes after pleading guilty at an eight-minute hearing to murdering his eighteen-year-old girl-friend, back in Cambridge Detective Chief Inspector Joe Breed was telling the court that before Hopkins was arrested foul play had not been suspected.

Breed and Detective Inspector Lilley spoke of their interview with Hopkins after his arrest. Of how he had been unable to remember where in Miss Wollner's room he had found the money, or whether he had thrown an eiderdown over her. He had also been unable to recall whether he had or had not struck his former landlady. To Lilley he had admitted that after returning frightened to his lodgings, 'I realized I must have done something.' In reply to Mr O'Connor, Inspector Lilley said that the substance of Hopkins' replies to the police questions was that he 'couldn't remember' what had happened.

After Mr Sutcliffe had read out to the court Hopkins' written statement in which he had tried to remember the events of 15 July leading to Miss Wollner's death, Mr O'Connor took the opportunity to briefly relate his client's disturbed and unhappy background. The defence was to rely on medical experts to satisfy the jury that Hopkins was suffering from diminished responsibility at the time he allegedly killed Cacilie Wollner, and would therefore not be subject to the death penalty. Mr O'Connor told the jury in his opening address that Hopkins had been born three months prematurely, resulting in brain injury. Over the years this had been exacerbated by other mental problems within his family. Whilst on remand in Brixton prison, Hopkins had been examined by three psychiatrists; the first of these was Dr Donald Webster, a consultant psychiatrist from Middlesbrough who had known Hopkins since he was twelve years old. He gave as his opinion that the accused was suffering from a psychopathic disorder, and that as recently as 1962, prior to his being sent to Borstal, he had suggested that special treatment in Broadmoor would be more appropriate. He had seen Hopkins while he had currently been on remand, and although he could find no evidence of psychosis, he considered that *his responsibility was substantially impaired.*

Dr Phillip Connell, a London psychiatric consultant who had at one time been in charge of the children's psychiatric welfare department in Newcastle took a similar view. He too had known Hopkins for several years, and told the court that after examining him seven years before he had recommended that he would be better away from his family environment. Dr Connell had also examined Hopkins whilst he had been in Brixton and had reached the conclusion that *his abnormal personality had substantially impaired his mental responsibility.*

The third expert, Dr T.N.C. Gibbons, reader in forensic psychiatry and consultant psychiatrist at Bethlem Royal and Maudsley Hospitals in London, was unequivocal. He said that after having examined Hopkins in Brixton prison, he was in no doubt that *he was suffering from an abnormality of the mind.* 'As a result of this abnormality of mind,' said Dr Gibbons, 'he is suffering from a mental abnormality which *substantially impairs his mental responsibility.*'

Mr O'Connor pressed home this point by asking, 'Whatever went on in Miss Wollner's room, in your opinion was his responsibility for what happened substantially impaired?'

'Yes, I am strongly of the opinion that it was *substantially impaired* at the time of the crime,' replied Dr Gibbons.

So far, so good, from the defence point of view: all three expert witnesses had remained unshaken in their assertions. However, when Dr Calder, principal medical officer at Brixton prison entered

the witness box, there was a slight hiccup. Although agreeing with
Mr O'Connor that Hopkins was suffering from an abnormality of
the mind, and that when under stress a man of his type would be
less responsible than at other times, he disagreed that the events
that had allegedly occurred in Miss Wollner's room were such as to
have put him under stress. He further dissented with the opinions
of the other medical witnesses who had stated that Hopkins'
mental responsibility was always impaired. Despite this difference
of opinion, Mr O'Connor was nevertheless quite satisfied with the
way the defence had gone.

Mr Sutcliffe in his closing speech to the jury reminded them that
they had to decide whether Hopkins had intended to kill Miss
Wollner, or do her serious harm whilst indifferent to the possible
consequences. If the defence had satisfied them that Hopkins was
suffering from an abnormality of the mind at the time he
committed the alleged offences, the verdict would be manslaughter. If on the other hand they were satisfied that he had
deliberately broken into Cacilie Wollner's house, and that as the
results of his acts towards her she had died of shock, he would be
guilty of murder. 'I suggest that the features of this case show the
ordinary actions of a perfectly ordinary burglar who was disturbed
by someone who could recognize, identify and give evidence
against him unless she was killed. If that is right, then your verdict
will be "guilty of murder" ', he told the jury.

In his closing speech Mr O'Connor homed-in on the undeniable
fact that without his statement there would almost certainly have
been no prosecution against Hopkins. He said there was very little
evidence to suggest that the accused had attacked Miss Wollner,
and even less that he had suffocated her with the eiderdown. After
referring again to his client's mental state, Mr O'Connor ended by
asking for either an acquittal, or alternatively a verdict of
manslaughter while suffering from diminished responsibility.

Had Hopkins' abnormality substantially impaired his mental
responsibility at the time of the alleged killing? That, said Mr
Justice Thesiger during his summing-up, was the question of 'vital
importance' in the case.

After four days of listening to arguments and submissions
concerning the state of Hopkins' mind at the time he allegedly
killed Cacilie Wollner, the jury had now only to listen to the
judge's final summary before retiring to consider their verdict.

The judge pointed out the danger inherent in the 'diminished responsibility' qualification if included in a guilty verdict; that it may encourage weak-minded individuals to forego exercising restraint in their actions if they believed that there was a good chance of their being held to be of diminished responsibility. He spoke about the degree of impairment, and whether it could be termed 'substantial' – ' ... a matter on which juries may quite legitimately differ from doctors', he said.

The judge briefly entered into semantics when defining the difference between inference and speculation. Referring to a defence submission he said, 'One cannot get rid of the responsibility for drawing a conclusion from the facts simply by calling it speculation ... ' – a good example of the shrewd insight Mr Justice Thesiger displayed in regard to both the prosecution and defence. He reminded the jury that Hopkins 'was under supervision for some time before the alleged crime', and that having already been to approved schools and borstals, he was treated 'as an ordinary troublesome fellow, and was not put out of circulation because he was substantially irresponsible to the point of being really insane.'

Finally, while upholding the right of Hopkins not to go into the witness box, he commented obliquely that an explanation to clarify matters might have been expected if a 'certain appearance' had been made out against a person.

Mr Justice Thesiger summed-up for an hour-and-a-half before sending the jury out to consider their verdict. Their deliberations took over two hours. As they returned Hopkins watched them, as emotionless as he had been throughout. Only as the foreman announced that they had found him guilty of manslaughter on the grounds of diminished responsibility, did he appear to relax slightly, as if in relief.

As he passed sentence Mr Justice Thesiger remarked that after breaking into Miss Wollner's house, 'Because he was of diminished responsibility he failed to control himself. He is therefore of greater danger to the public than someone who has control of himself and does not choose to do so', a paradoxical situation as an individual such as the judge described would have qualified for the death sentence. In sentencing Hopkins to life imprisonment, he said that such an indeterminate sentence ' ... will best protect the public, providing those responsible for his custody do not consider releasing him until they think that it is safe to do so'.

As Rhys Llewelyn Hopkins disappeared from view to start his life sentence, and counsel gathered together their papers, few probably took time off to reflect on how near he had come to the gallows. Certainly the trial, which was very soon forgotten, had attracted minimal press and television interest, only the local Cambridge papers covering it in any depth. This was no doubt due to its lack of sensationalism. No sexual undertones, nothing unusually sadistic about the attack on Miss Wollner or in her mode of death, and little that was newsworthy in either his manner of capture – he had surrendered himself to a uniformed policeman on routine patrol – or in the investigation and questioning that followed.

The trial itself had largely been confined to medical opinions as to Hopkins' state of mind, hardly the stuff to fire the public's imagination. Nevertheless, in my view the Hopkins trial epitomized British justice at its best. An array of distinguished medical and legal experts giving their erudite opinions as to the accused person's mental condition, followed by a peerless summing-up by one of Her Majesty's judges, after which twelve fellow citizens arrived at their carefully considered judgement.

As a result of that judgement, the twenty-one-year-old hotel worker, one of life's unfortunates from birth, who had spoken scarcely half-a-dozen words throughout his trial, left the Assize court to begin a life sentence, but with the shadow of the hangman's noose removed. At another time, or in another place, he may well not have been so fortunate.

# 8   Ellough's Wartime Slaying, Suffolk 1944

With only four rain-free days, November 1944 was the wettest month in Britain for four years. Despite the bad weather at home, across the Channel the war in Europe was entering its final phase; five months after D-Day Allied troops were making substantial inroads into Hitler's European fortress.

In the air the protagonists were each still striving to dominate the skies, whilst wreaking maximum havoc on the ground. The night of 8/9 November was no exception. Following daylight raids by bombers of the United States Eighth Air Force and RAF Bomber Command on German oil installations at Merseburg and Bad Homberg, Mosquito light bombers were striking during the night at Herford and Hannover. At home a flying-bomb attack had been launched against the east coast. Several were destroyed, but others penetrated the defences to fall inland causing considerable damage and some casualties.

One person that night however, fell victim not to enemy action, but at the hands of one of her own countrymen.

Winifred Mary Evans was a twenty-seven-year-old unmarried girl from Harlesden in west London. Two years previously she had enlisted in the Women's Auxiliary Air Force (WAAF), and at the time of her death she was serving as a wireless operator at the RAF airfield at Ellough, near Beccles in Suffolk.

Winnie Evans was a pleasant, reserved girl with a code of morals that discouraged casual wartime romances. As a friend said at the time, 'If anyone tried to get fresh with her she used to slap them.'

She had been dogged with sadness throughout the war. Both her parents had died, and a brother had been killed in the Western Desert. Despite these tragedies she enjoyed service life and had many friends.

On the evening of Wednesday, 8 November 1944, with several other young servicewomen, Winnie attended a dance at one of the many American air force bases in the area. The girls had an enjoyable evening's dancing with their hosts, so-much-so that she was surprised when she noticed the time and realized that she was going to be late back for her spell of duty, due to start at 11.30 p.m.

Together with her friend, Corporal Margaret Johns, she left the dance and hurried back to Ellough. There, after changing into her working uniform, she donned her greatcoat against the bitter cold and set off along the mile-long, pitch black lane to the base headquarters. Corporal Johns offered to accompany her at least part of the way, but Winnie declined the offer.

After her friend had left, Margaret Johns went across to the girls' ablutions hut. Switching on the light she was startled to see a man in RAF uniform standing unsteadily in the lobby. It was apparent that the intruder had had too much to drink, but seeing that he was junior in rank to herself, the WAAF corporal had no hesitation in challenging him. 'What are you doing here?' she asked.

'I'm lost, isn't this No 1 site?' the airman replied.

'No, this is the WAAF site, so get out,' she ordered.

'Will you show me the way out as I'm drunk and can't see?' Corporal Johns obliged, showing him out and pointing out the road he should take back to his own quarters. Before setting out the airman made a final clumsy and obvious pass at the corporal saying, 'Can I thank you?'

'No, get down the road,' she replied. She watched as he started off in the same direction as that taken by her friend Winifred Evans a few minutes earlier.

The airman discovered by Corporal Johns was Arthur Heys, a thirty-seven-year-old leading aircraftsman, married with a young family, from Colne in Lancashire. Heys had also been to a dance on that fateful evening, in Beccles, the small market town a couple of miles down the road. He too had enjoyed himself, dancing and drinking with the local girls, although his pleasure had been dampened when upon leaving the dance he discovered that his pedal cycle was missing. It meant that he had to walk back to his camp.

No one knows what thoughts passed through Heys' mind that night as he made his unsteady way along the road leading to the aerodrome. Perhaps it was loneliness (he had only returned from leave four days previously), inflamed by alcohol that directed his track to the women's quarters and their ablutions hut where maybe he was hoping to find a willing partner prepared to indulge in a brief, nocturnal sexual adventure. If so he was soon to be disappointed.

What happened during the next half-hour can only be conjecture. Whether Winifred Evans became aware of the person following her – perhaps even waiting for him to catch up, glad to have company on the lonely road – or whether Heys saw the lone girl ahead and caught up with her unawares, is not known. What is indisputable is that the two met on that cold, dark country lane, and that Winnie Evans, the virtuous, fun-loving girl from London, met a savage, violent death. The absence of any signs of a prolonged struggle suggested that she remained unsuspecting until the moment she was attacked. She then either fell or was thrown into a ditch where she was frenziedly assaulted and raped, during the course of which she died as her assailant pushed her face hard into the mud at the bottom of the ditch.

It was there at eight o'clock the next morning that Claude Fiske, an electrician's mate, found her as he cycled along Ellough Road past Green Lane on the way to work. A brief glance told him that the girl lying in the ditch was dead, so hurrying on to work he telephoned Beccles police station to tell of his grim find.

Detective Inspector G.A. Read who, from pounding the Beccles beat twenty years earlier, had risen to become the head of East Suffolk CID, was immediately notified and set off at once for the scene. The nature and ferocity of the attack, together with the large number of potential suspects among the British and allied servicemen stationed in the area, the local civilian population and the Italian prisoners-of-war in a nearby camp, persuaded Read to send for the assistance of Scotland Yard.

While the Yard officers were travelling up from London, Read and his men carefully searched the scene and were rewarded when Inspector Bill Bryant found a jigger button, similar to those attached to RAF greatcoats, lying near the body. Other local officers interviewed and took written statements from likely witnesses, Corporal Johns included.

East Anglia had been in the front line since the outbreak of the war. In the early months its long sandy beaches had been considered inviting landing places for Hitler's invasion fleet, so hundreds of concrete pill boxes and other defences, on and offshore, had been constructed in preparation for the anticipated assault.

As the invasion threat had receded, much of the countryside had been transformed into a vast airfield, at first for the RAF and later for the American Eighth Air Force. Ellough's brief history had followed a reverse course; built in 1943 specifically for the arrival of the Americans, it was taken over by the RAF during the following year.

Despite these outward manifestations of the war, much of the day-to-day life in the region continued as it had done in peacetime. While in the United States the ailing President Franklin D. Roosevelt was being elected for the fourth term, the *Eastern Daily Press* on Friday, 10 November, was largely devoted to the annual mayoral elections that had taken place locally the previous day. The parochial church council at Blyford reported that the church restoration fund had received £17.0.8d. (£17.03) from a dance at Holton school, whilst on the Wednesday at Downham Market town hall, over five hundred assorted exhibits had crowded into the District Poultry and Rabbit Show.

It was to this combined air of militarism and peaceful normality, seemingly unaffected by the war, that Detective Chief Inspector Ted Greeno, Detective Sergeant Hodge and the Home Office pathologist, Doctor Keith Simpson, arrived just before midnight on Thursday. The three men were met by Read, who acquainted them with the known facts before taking them to the scene where the body of Winnie Evans, covered by a tarpaulin and shrouded in a light covering of snow, still lay as she had been found earlier in the day.

After Simpson had made a preliminary examination of the body at the scene, Greeno directed that it be removed to the nearby Beccles Hospital in readiness for a later post-mortem. There followed through the night several hours of intensive police activity, with Greeno himself setting the example by interviewing dozens of Italian prisoners-of-war at a nearby camp, while Suffolk officers concentrated their efforts at No 1 site, that referred to by the intruder encountered by Corporal Johns.

Later in the day Greeno struck upon the idea of asking Corporal Johns to watch discreetly the pay parade due to take place at No 1 site, in the hope that she would pick out the airman with whom she had exchanged words two nights previously. He was not disappointed; the young WAAF watched as successive airmen marched up to the pay table to receive their money. 'That's him,' she said to Detective Constable Bedingfield, the Lowestoft detective by her side, as Heys stepped forward. The policeman stopped the airman as he walked away from the parade and told him that his presence was required at Beccles police station for questioning in connection with the murder of aircraftswoman Evans.

Meanwhile in Beccles Hospital, a post-mortem performed by Dr Simpson, assisted by Dr Biddle, the county pathologist, confirmed that Winifred Evans had suffocated as the result of her head being pushed into the mud at the bottom of the ditch while she was being raped.

The first thing Greeno noticed as Heys stood before him was a tear in his greatcoat from which a jigger button was missing. During his investigations earlier, Greeno had interviewed many of the airmen from No 1 site, and had been told by hut mates of Heys that after his evening out on Wednesday, he had not returned to his bed until the early hours of Thursday morning. He had then risen before reveille a few hours later in order to clean his shoes and uniform undisturbed. Although such behaviour was suspicious, it was far from conclusive. Greeno knew that much would depend on his interrogation of the suspect.

Heys was at a disadvantage from the start of his interview with the detective, being unaware of how much evidence he had already gathered. Like most other personnel at the airfield he was undoubtedly aware that investigators from London had arrived at Beccles less than twenty-four hours before, so he was probably trying to convince himself that they had not had enough time to obtain any significant clues pointing to himself. But could he be sure? What traces, if any, had he left at the scene? Had anything subsequently come to light that could connect him with Winifred Evans? Although he had not been incapably drunk on Wednesday night, his mind had been befuddled and he could not remember with certainty the exact sequence of events that had taken place.

In the written statement that he eventually agreed to make, Heys said that he had returned to the camp by the most direct route from Beccles, and arrived at his billet at about 12.30 a.m. After further questioning by Greeno, he admitted that he had stopped off at the WAAF site, where he had been discovered by Corporal Johns. This was as much as he would concede; he emphatically denied arriving back at his billet later than the time he had stated, or rising early in the morning to clean his uniform and shoes.

At the end of the interview, after agreeing to provide a sample of his hair for examination and comparison, Heys was allowed to leave the police station to return to his camp. Greeno was satisfied that Heys was the man he was after, but the circumstantial evidence so far gathered, and Heys statement completely denying any involvement in the crime, made it imperative that the Yard man obtain additional evidence directly linking Heys with the attack before he could arrest him.

Such evidence was not long in forthcoming. Upon returning to his billet, Heys was dismayed to find that the police had been there during his absence and had taken away the tunic, trousers and shoes he had been wearing on the night Winifred Evans died.

Over three weeks elapsed before Heys and Greeno faced each other again. In the meantime grieving friends and relations gathered at the funeral of Winnie Evans, which took place on 16 December at All Saints Church in Harlesden.

Not far away at the Metropolitan Police forensic laboratory, Dr Simpson was examining Heys uniform and shoes seized by the police. What the items revealed to Dr Simpson, who was again assisted by Dr Biddle, was later to play a vital part in securing a conviction against Heys. Brick dust found on his shoes was similar to that discovered on the murdered woman's shoes, and in the ditch where she had lain. Despite cleaning attempts, stains on Heys' uniform were revealed as blood; specks of mud were found on his tunic, and most significantly, human hair discovered on his uniform was said by Simpson to have most likely come from the body of Winifred Evans.

By Simpson's own exacting standards the evidence was not conclusive. The bloodstains were too weak to be grouped, while it was just possible that the hair could have come from someone other than Winnie Evans.

Nevertheless Greeno, while aware of Simpson's unwillingness to compromise his professional opinion and judgement, submitted all the evidence now available to the Director of Public Prosecutions for him to decide whether Heys should be arrested and charged with the murder.

The DPP did not long delay his decision that the prosecution should go ahead. Thus it was that on Tuesday, 5 December 1944, Arthur Heys was again confronted at Beccles police station by the three detectives who had worked so hard and painstakingly to orchestrate the meeting. It was to be the last day of freedom for the thirty-seven-year-old Lancashire airman.

Greeno lost no time at their second meeting. After briefly reintroducing Hodge and Read, he said to Heys, 'I am not satisfied that you have told the truth with regard to your movements on that night. You will be detained in connection with the murder.' For several minutes Heys sat without replying as the policemen waited patiently. Eventually the airman raised his head and addressing Greeno said, 'I have been thinking, I can't see what evidence you have to connect me with it. Can't you tell me?'

'No,' replied Greeno, 'not at this stage.'

Later the same evening, in the presence of the detectives, Heys was formally charged with the murder of Winifred Mary Evans. After a short pause the accused man replied, 'I didn't do it.'

After being charged Heys was transferred to a cell in the police station to spend the night pending his appearance at a specially convened court the following morning.

The first night spent in custody after having been charged with a serious offence is almost invariably one of loneliness, apprehension and often despair. For Heys, knowing that soon he would be going on trial for his life, such feelings must have been exaggerated to an unbearable degree. For over two hours he sat alone contemplating his situation and speculating on his future. Eventually he went across to his cell door.

Police Constable Harold Twite, charged with the duty of remaining in the corridor outside Heys' cell overnight, was surprised to hear the airman remark conversationally to him through the cell door wicket, 'I wonder what clue they have got? They must have something.' Twite told him that he was forbidden to discuss the case, at the same time reminding him that he had earlier been cautioned. Undeterred, Heys persisted in trying to engage the policeman in conversation. 'What time did the murder take place?' he asked. Twite told him that he didn't know, whereupon Heys endeavoured to enlighten him, 'I have seen by the papers that it was round about half-past-twelve. I was there round about twenty-past-twelve.' He must have immediately realized that this last remark was indiscreet and potentially very damaging, especially when made to a policeman, for he quickly followed it up by saying, 'I didn't ought to have made a statement at all. Let me see – it's one, two, three, four that I have made.' He then lapsed into a pensive silence, discouraged from making further remarks by his unresponsive gaoler. As it was he was unaware that Twite had carefully noted his comments in his pocket-book, and was later to quote them at the airman's trial.

The next morning, Wednesday, 6 December 1944, four weeks exactly from the night Winifred Evans died, the man accused of her murder made his first court appearance. The presiding magistrate, Mr S.J. Hindes, after listening to evidence of Heys' arrest, acceded to Greeno's request for a remand until 15 December. There were to be two further remands until on Wednesday, 10 January 1945, Mr H.J. Parham for the prosecution, stood up to present the case for the Crown. In the meantime Heys was to spend the festive season in Norwich prison.

Christmas and the New Year are especially harrowing for men in prison. Separated from their families and all the other people and places they hold dear, inmates have time to dwell on their misfortune, which in turn often leads to periods of deep depression. To alleviate this the regime nowadays is relaxed slightly over the festive season. Seasonal fare, albeit canned and frozen is served, and in addition to the television and video that is normally available, competitions and other activities are organized. Christmas 1944 was different; after four years of war food was still strictly rationed, and prison regimes generally were more austere and autocratic than is the case more than forty years later.

For Heys, married with three young children, the festive period must have been a time of poignant memories and bitter regret and recrimination. The only relief from his thoughts and forebodings were the visits from his wife, who arrived at Norwich exhausted after the tortuous, wartime rail journey from her home in Lancashire.

It was probably during the remand period that Heys conceived the ruse that he hoped might save him.

The court was packed when the committal proceedings opened on 10 January, and for the next two days the spectators, including the wife and brother of the accused man, listened in the Beccles courtroom as Mr Parham outlined his case and called his witnesses.

The Crown counsel described the alleged sequence of events leading up to the discovery of Winifred Evans's body in the Ellough ditch. Heys sat impassively as counsel detailed the injuries that had been inflicted on the young airwoman, and the manner of her death. As Mr Parham continued it became apparent that the Crown case, although largely circumstantial, was a formidable one. After concluding his résumé of the case he started to call his witnesses, twenty-three in all on the first day.

Among the first was John Roberts, the dead girl's brother-in-law who described her as 'a rather reserved type' who had been in the WAAF for about two years.

Next, Heys listened attentively as Corporal Margaret Johns told the court of their encounter on the WAAF site shortly after midnight on the night her friend died.

Following Corporal Johns into the witness box stepped two former hut mates of Heys. Leading Aircraftsman Victor Redmonds said that Heys had returned to his billet between 1 a.m. and 1.30 a.m. on the Thursday morning without switching on the light. Later that morning he noticed that Heys' shoes were unusually dirty. The observant airman had also taken note of scratches on Heys' hands. Redmonds added that the murder was the chief topic of conversation that evening, although he remembered that Heys had not joined in the general discussion.

Another airman, Reginald Hunter, testified that a few days after the murder he was discussing it with Heys, who casually mentioned that at the time it was being committed he must have been on a corner some thirty yards away, adding that at the time visibility was only half that distance. In the light of Hunter's evidence it would seem that Heys, who at the time of this conversation had already been questioned by Greeno, was belatedly attempting to explain away his presence in the immediate vicinity at the time Winifred Evans was being attacked.

On the second day of the police court hearing another eight witnesses gave their evidence, including Detective Constable Bedingfield, who was present when Heys was identified by Corporal Johns on the pay parade, and Police Constable Twite, who recounted the brief but significant utterances made by Heys whilst he was in the cell at Beccles police station after having been charged.

There was an expectant stir in court as Detective Chief Inspector Ted Greeno was called to the witness box. All those present listened intently as the well-known Scotland Yard detective took the oath and prepared to testify.

In reply to Mr Parham, Greeno told the court that he had been in charge of the investigation since his arrival in Beccles at midnight on Thursday, 9 November 1944. He went on to describe the immediate enquiries that had been set in hand, mentioning the jigger button that had been found at the scene, and concluded with his interviews with the suspect, during the first of which he noticed the damage to the airman's greatcoat which had a similar button missing. Greeno's evidence was given in the unemotional, self-assured manner befitting a senior-ranking, experienced detective. As he stepped down from the witness box with not a glance at the accused, no one in court, with the possible exception of Heys, could fail to have been impressed by the account he had given of the police investigation, and the subsequent interrogation of Heys that had led to his arrest.

Towards the end of the second day's hearing, Dr Biddle, pathologist at the East Suffolk and Ipswich Hospital, gave evidence of the post-mortem. The doctor told the court that he had taken a sample of Heys' blood, which upon analysis proved to be of a different group to that of Winifred Evans. He said that he had also found four human hairs identical to samples from the head of the murdered woman. However, the doctor was later to agree under cross-examination at the trial that the hairs found, which were among many found on Heys' clothing, were of a common type similar to those that grew on the heads of thousands of women.

Dr Biddle continued by testifying that a bloodstain found on Heys' apparently recently cleaned and pressed uniform appeared to belong to Winifred Evans's blood group, and that the mud and dust found on his shoes was similar to that at the bottom of the ditch where the body was found. The doctor carefully avoided making positive assertions when testifying, confining himself to similarities and probabilities.

The county pathologist was the last important witness to be called. Soon afterwards the prosecution concluded its case, with Mr Alpe, representing Heys, reserving his client's defence. The court chairman, Major Blower, then committed Heys for trial at the forthcoming Suffolk Assizes, due to commence at Bury St Edmunds eight days later.

When Greeno returned to Beccles police station he was given a letter that had been received earlier by the Commanding Officer of Heys' squadron. With considerable interest Greeno read the contents:

> 'Will you please give this letter to the solicitors for the airman who is so wrongfully accused of murdering Winnie Evans? I want to state I am responsible for the above-mentioned girl's death. I had arranged to meet her at the bottom of the road

where the body was found, at midnight. When I arrived she was not there. I waited some time, and decided to walk down towards the WAAF quarters. Just before I reached this I heard a voice and stood close to the hedge. I heard footsteps. It proved to be an airman. I don't think he saw me. I then saw someone I recognized was Winnie. She said I should not have come down to meet her. A WAAF friend had offered to go along with her, as the airman ahead was drunk and had lost his way. She had her bicycle with her; no one will ever find this ...'

The writer concluded by saying that he had destroyed his clothes, and that he would soon be going overseas.

Although the author of the letter had asked that it be given to the defence solicitors, the Squadron Commander had quite rightly handed it to the police instead. The defence in any event would be informed of the letter and advised of its contents.

In the meantime Greeno had just over a week to trace the letter's origin. One line it contained was enough to satisfy him that it was the work of the accused, ' ... A WAAF friend had offered to go along with her, as the airman ahead was drunk and had lost his way ...' Who else could have known of the drunken airman who was lost apart from the airman himself and Corporal Johns? Winnie Evans had departed for duty before her friend had suddenly come upon the airman, so she could not possibly have known.

The question posed for Greeno was not 'who' had written the letter, but 'how' had it come to be written and then posted whilst the accused was on remand in Norwich prison? Assuming he was able to find satisfactory answers to both questions, he would still have to convince the jury.

The detective went to Norwich prison where he soon established that a blue pencil similar to the one used to write the letter was available to inmates, and that there would be little difficulty in arranging for a letter to be smuggled out and posted. Having satisfied himself that the letter could have been written and dispatched by Heys, Greeno set about proving that his man had indeed written it. Among the accused's property taken possession of by police was a watch with a tab affixed bearing hand-printed instructions to a repairer. Greeno also obtained several leave applications made by Heys, all written in block capitals. Now all but certain that the letter had come from Heys, Greeno was nonetheless aware that he himself was not a handwriting expert, and that an astute defence lawyer would certainly capitalize on that during cross-examination. He therefore sent the letter for examination by Detective Chief Superintendent Fred Cherrill, head of Scotland Yard's Fingerprint Bureau.

Although Cherrill had built up his reputation as a fingerprint expert, as he explains in his autobiography, ' ... fingerprints and handwriting have something in common. A fingerprint possesses a host of intricate and minute details. So does handwriting, if one has the ability to detect them.'

Cherrill had that ability, and after studying the letter and comparing its printing with that of the repair tab and the leave applications, the similarities he found left him in no doubt that the examples had been written by the same man.

The trial of Arthur Heys before Mr Justice McNaughten, opened at Bury St Edmunds on Monday, 22 January 1945, and lasted for three days.

Mr John Flowers, prosecuting, pointed out to the jury at the outset that the case against the accused was largely circumstantial, but the cumulative effect of the evidence he said, pointed unerringly to Heys as the man who had slain Winifred Evans the previous November. Heys was to rely largely for his defence on the letter purportedly written by another, anonymous airman confessing to the crime.

The court on the Monday morning was crowded, among the spectators being Heys' wife, by her presence still loyally supporting her husband as he faced the greatest ordeal of his life.

After his opening address, Mr Flowers called his witnesses, who repeated the evidence they had earlier given at the committal proceedings. Each was cross-examined by Mr Alpe without any of them materially altering their testimony. Mr Justice McNaughten interrupted on one occasion, after he had heard evidence that brick dust had been found on the soles of Heys' shoes, to ask that a plan of the aerodrome showing the route of a mud covered path of red brick be made available to the court. The drama was to come the following day.

The next morning, after brief evidence of receipt of the anonymous letter at the aerodrome had been given, Mr Flowers called Greeno to the witness box. The policeman produced the letter, written in block capitals with a blue crayon pencil, together with the watch tab bearing Heys' printed instructions. Greeno told the court that similar pencils to that used to write the letter were available to the inmates of Norwich prison, and went on to describe the method whereby a letter could be smuggled out of the gaol and then posted.

After Greeno the court heard from Detective Chief Superintendent Fred Cherrill. Counsel on both sides were acutely aware that the evidence tendered by the stockily-built, white-haired policeman could largely determine the outcome of the trial, and with it Heys' fate.

After a few preliminary questions, Mr Flowers asked the crucial one: 'What is your opinion on the anonymous letter; was it or was it not written by the same person who printed the letters on the leave forms and on the watch tab?' Cherrill replied without hesitation, 'It was the same person.'

'Have you any doubt about it at all?' asked Mr Flowers.

'No sir.' Counsel pressed home the point, 'If the other ones were written by the prisoner, so was the anonymous letter?'

'Yes,' replied Cherrill.

'Thank you, Superintendent.' As Mr Flowers sat down Heys must have realized that his scheme had been exposed, and that his defence to the charge was now all but hopeless.

Mr Alpe did his best; he cross-examined the fingerprint expert cleverly and at considerable length concerning the formation of the characters that made up the letter. He concentrated on the differences rather than on the similarities between the capitals used in the letter and those on the watch tab and leave application forms. Asked to explain the apparent dissimilarity between many of the letters, Cherrill explained that they could have occurred either as a result of the haste with which they were written or as a deliberate attempt by the writer to disguise his hand. He ended by saying that in his opinion some of the letters were 'superficially different, but basically not'.

Apart from a couple of minor witnesses, Cherrill's evidence ended the prosecution case. Sound but not spectacular can best describe it, although to the defence it presented a formidable challenge.

As Heys stepped into the witness box to testify on his own behalf, all in court were aware that if he was to escape the gallows he had to cast doubt in the jury's mind on the reliability of the prosecution's expert witnesses and their evidence. The task was daunting; nonetheless Heys, who had maintained his composure throughout the trial, answered the questions put to him by Mr Alpe, confidently. He admitted as much as he dare, being particularly careful not to dispute the evidence of Corporal Margaret Johns as to their confrontation in the WAAF's ablutions hut. He reaffirmed that it was as the result of having lost his way that he inadvertently found himself in the women's part of the base.

He explained that his visit to Beccles on the evening of the murder was the first time he had been out of the camp since returning from ten days home-leave spent with his family. Heys said that he had drunk about eight pints of beer during the evening before going to the dance. Upon leaving he found his bicycle was missing, so he had no option but to return to his camp on foot. It was whilst he was so doing, he said, that he lost his way.

He continued by telling the court that at the time he was under the impression that he had reached his own site, as he was unaware that more than one road led from Beccles to the RAF station. Heys insisted that after receiving directions from Corporal Johns, he returned straightaway to his own hut, arriving there at about 12.30 a.m. He explained that the reason for not switching on the light in his hut was because he thought his pals were asleep, and it was not the custom to turn on the light unless one was on duty.

The airman denied that he had even seen, let alone caught up with Winifred Evans on the night she died. To the question put by Mr Alpe, 'Did you kill Winnie Evans?' he replied clearly, 'I did not.'

'And you never wrote this anonymous letter?'

'No sir,' Heys replied.

He showed no signs of nervousness as Mr Flowers stood up to cross-examine him; in any event there was time for only a few preliminary, innocuous questions before the court adjourned at the end of the second day.

When Mr Flowers resumed his cross-examination on the Wednesday morning, he soon got around to asking Heys some very pertinent questions. 'How do you account for the blood on the tunic?' he asked. 'The only reason I can give is that on one occasion I went out with two men and one cut his hand in falling off a cycle and I helped him to get up. It would be last October,' was Heys' reply.

Mr Flowers moved on to the anonymous letter. After reading out the sentences that referred to the writer allegedly meeting Winifred Evans, and her reference to the drunken airman ahead who had lost his way, he put to Heys, 'Do you see that the writer is purporting to say the poor girl came along and told him that her friend had offered to come along with her, as an airman ahead had lost his way and was drunk?'

'I should not know anything about that,' answered Heys.

'But you were the airman who had lost his way,' Mr Flowers pressed him, 'How could anyone else in the world have the knowledge to put it in this letter but you?'

'I did not write the letter,' Heys stubbornly insisted.

Despite his persistent denials, it was the letter above all else that incriminated him in Winifred Evans's murder. As he returned to the dock Arthur Heys knew that only a miracle could now save him. What he had conceived as a brilliant ruse aimed at diverting suspicion from himself, had succeeded only in reinforcing the case against him. Without the letter the Crown would have had to rely almost entirely on circumstantial evidence, which although strong, was not conclusive. One can only speculate on the possible outcome of the trial had not evidence of the anonymous letter been introduced.

There remained only the closing speeches and the judge's summing-up. All three followed a predictable course; Mr Flowers emphasized to the jury the evidence of the letter, telling them that, 'If anything else was needed to prove the case against the accused, it was provided by the anonymous letter.' After reading again the extract he had earlier quoted stating that a WAAF friend had offered to go along with Miss Evans as a drunken airman was ahead, Mr Flowers continued, 'Nobody in the world could have put that in this letter according to any reasonable view of this evidence except this man.'

When it came to Mr Alpe's turn he opened by quoting Richelieu, 'Give me a dozen lines by the hand of the most innocent man, and I will find something therein which will cause him to hang.' He went on by appealing to the jury's incredulity: 'It had been suggested that the letter had been smuggled out of prison. Would a man charged with murder be wandering about the prison? Letters from prisoners were on official paper. Was it suggested he had accomplices in prison?' Mr Alpe asked. He reminded the jury that speculation or suspicion was not enough, pointing out that the evidence was all circumstantial and far from conclusive.

The summing-up by Mr Justice McNaughten was later favourably commented upon by the Appeal Court. The judge made clear at the beginning of his address to the jury his revulsion at the crime which he described as, 'a murder more savage and horrible than any in my experience of crime'. He then went on to review carefully the three days of evidence. As has been seen much of this was circumstantial, but this in no way detracted from its value. Before sending the jury out to consider their verdict, Mr Justice McNaughten gave them a final reminder that if they believed the statement made by the accused to the police to be true, he was entitled to be acquitted.

The jury evidently thought otherwise, for a mere forty minutes after retiring they were back in court, where the foreman announced that they had found Heys guilty. When asked by the clerk if he had any reason to give why sentence of death should not be passed on him, Heys replied, 'God knows I am innocent of this foul crime. I know God will look after me. I am not afraid.'

As Heys turned to leave the court after being sentenced, the only sound was the quiet sobbing of his wife in the public gallery. He glanced briefly at the woman who had sat in court throughout both the hearing at the police court and at his trial, before disappearing from sight.

On 26 February 1945, Heys' appeal was summarily rejected, Mr Justice Humphreys remarking that, 'The victim of the murder was a young lady. She had been outraged and murdered by some man who had behaved worse than any beast ... The jury heard all the evidence and convicted after a fair, full, accurate and, on the whole, favourable summing-up, and there was no ground upon which the court could interfere with the verdict.'

The agony of Arthur Heys was to last another fifteen days following the rejection of his appeal. Shortly after 8 a.m. on Tuesday, 13 March, a notice was affixed to the main gate of Norwich prison announcing that 'Judgement of death was this day executed on Arthur Heys in our presence'. It was signed Mr Thomas Wilson, Under-Sheriff of Suffolk, Mr A.A. Rice, Justice of the Peace for the City of Norwich, Mr Sidney T.E.P. Ennion, Governor of the prison, and the Rev. S. Merrifield, the prison chaplain. It was the first execution to be carried out at Norwich since Walter Smith, a general labourer of Stroud in Kent, was hanged on 8 March 1938 for the murder of Albert Edward Baker on a barge at Felixstowe.

So was enacted the final scene in what after all was a sordid, sexually motivated killing that attracted little interest in the newspapers of the day.

Momentous events were taking place elsewhere as the war entered its final months, while at home two other murders attracted the public's attention. Running concurrently with Heys' trial was that of a twenty-two-year-old American paratrooper, Karl Gustav Hulten, and his eighteen-year-old accomplice, Elizabeth Maud Jones, both convicted and sentenced to death for the murder of hire car driver George Edward Heath in what became known as the 'Cleft Chin' murder. Jones was later reprieved, but the sentence on Hulten was carried out.

On the day of Heys' execution, a twenty-six-year-old labourer, Ronald Hedley, was sentenced to death at the Old Bailey, and his co-accused Thomas James Jenkins (older brother of Charles Jenkins, executed two years later for his part in the de Antiquis murder), was sentenced to eight years imprisonment for the killing of Captain Ralph Binney, who died after being struck and dragged along for over a mile after he had tried to stop the men's getaway car following a smash-and-grab raid in the City of London. A memorial medal named after Captain Binney was later struck, to be awarded annually for the greatest act of heroism in support of law and order.

Nonetheless the Heys case was noteworthy for three things; the speed with which the investigation – despite there being hundreds of suspects – resulted in the arrest of the culprit; the forensic evidence which placed Heys at the scene of the crime as surely as if he had been seen there, and his abortive attempt to divert suspicion from himself by means of the anonymous letter. The first two points are not surprising in view of the detective, medical and legal talent assigned to solving the case, and later proving it in court. Greeno and Simpson were already household names in the field of murder investigation, and both were to further enhance their reputations in later years. The Suffolk county pathologist, Dr Eric Biddle, who was also involved in the investigation and gave evidence at the trial, sadly died a few months later.

The letter, however, was a different matter. It is arguable as to whether the combined efforts of the policemen and the pathologists would have been enough to secure a conviction had not Heys conceived the idea of writing a letter and having it smuggled out of prison. He grossly underestimated the deductive reasoning ability of those into whose hands the letter was to fall and who immediately spotted the elementary mistakes he had made in disclosing facts that could have been known only to the perpetrator of the crime. This miscalculation on his part sealed his eventual fate as effectively as did the hangman three months later.

# 9   Double Death at Stanfield Hall, Norfolk 1848

Good people pay attention and listen unto me,
Whilst I relate the awful facts of this horrid tragedy;
'Twas at a place called Stanfield Hall, not far from
   Wymondham town,
An ancient and a noble seat for many ages known.

There dwelt a learned gentleman and Jermy was his name,
Who of Norwich was recorder, and as such had great fame;
And with his son, a virtuous man, both met a dreadful end,
For both were shot one evening by a wicked murdering fiend.

Anon.

In 1848, James Blomfield Rush, tenant farmer, auctioneer and
estate agent of Potash Farm on the Stanfield Estate near
Wymondham, was in deep financial trouble.

The situation in which he found himself had its origins eleven
years earlier when his landlord, Isaac Jermy, an Oxford-educated
lawyer who had been appointed Recorder of Norwich in 1831, had
inherited from his father the Stanfield Hall estate, an inheritance
disputed by other members of the family. The resentment had
simmered over the years, and in September 1848 the Hall was
besieged by one of the claimants, John Larner, a cousin, who with
about eighty supporters burst into and ransacked the building.
The 4th Dragoon Guards had to be called in to restore order.

At the time that he had inherited the property in 1837, Isaac
Jermy had increased the rental of two farms on the estate which
had been leased to James Blomfield Rush by Jermy's late father.
The following year an extraordinary transaction took place

between Rush and Jermy. The former bought Potash Farm by means of a ten year mortgage granted by Jermy and ending on 30 November 1848. This apparent generosity on Jermy's part in fact bound Rush even more securely to him, in debt to Jermy as he now was for three farms on the estate.

In 1843, Rush's wife died leaving him with nine children, and the following year his father also died after accidentally shooting himself. It was suggested that Rush may have had a hand in the accident, but the matter was not pursued. Rush promptly borrowed from his father's estate money that had been left to his mother, thereby temporarily relieving some of the financial pressure.

Two years later in 1846, Rush decided to employ a governess for his children, so in October that year he advertised for one in *The Times*. As a result Emily Sandford, a young London girl, entered his employ after she and her parents had satisfied themselves as to his background and credentials. Not many months were to pass before Mr and Mrs Sandford and their daughter became aware of the deceptions Rush had perpetrated to enlist the services of Emily.

For the first few months all went well. Emily moved into Stanfield Hall Farm and adapted well to her duties as governess, considering herself fortunate to have obtained a post with such an upright and God-fearing man. Rush found himself increasingly attracted to the young woman, several years his junior, who now occupied the farm with him. He carefully kept from her knowledge of his own illegitimacy, his early brushes with the law, and an unfortunate episode seven years earlier when he had been sued for seduction and breach of promise. The suit had gone against him and had done nothing to aid his ailing finances.

With Emily Sandford the difficulties posed by having, as before, a legal wife in the background did not exist, so he was able to secure her seduction on the promise of marriage without qualms. After they had become lovers, Rush decided that it would be more convenient, and possibly less embarrassing, if Emily lived away from the farm. He therefore obtained lodgings for her in Islington, a district of London with which he was familiar. There he was able to visit her regularly under the guise of being her uncle, whilst remaining unhindered to grapple with the problems that were increasingly occupying him back in Norfolk.

James Rush's duplicity is amply illustrated by a series of

documents he prepared in October 1848. In the first of these, after a meeting at Emily Sandford's lodgings at Islington with old Thomas Jermy and the Larners, father and son, the three principal claimants to the Stanfield Hall estate, Rush agreed to do all possible to facilitate their obtaining possession of the estate, in return for which, if their claim was successful, he would retain his lease on the two farms he already worked for a further twenty-one years. This document was written by Emily from a copy supplied by Rush, and was duly signed by the claimants, with Emily witnessing the signatures.

Two days later at Rush's bidding, she travelled to Norwich where she was met by him and taken to Potash Farm. There they remained until the following Tuesday, 10 October, when she returned to Norwich and stayed in various inns and lodgings. During the next three-and-a-half weeks Rush visited Emily and asked her to copy for him other documents for Isaac Jermy to sign at Stanfield Hall. Later, with some misgivings, Emily signed the papers as a witness. They were remarkable documents; the first two extended the leases on the Felmingham and Stanfield Hall farms for a further twelve years, and the mortgage on Potash Farm for another three years beyond its expiry date on 28 November 1848 – a date that would soon be upon Rush. The third document was the most extraordinary of all and superseded the previous two. In return for Rush giving up all claim to the Felmingham and Stanfield Hall farms, and of doing everything possible to ensure that Isaac Jermy kept their possession, the latter in turn would relinquish all further mortgage claim on Potash Farm and would re-lease the Felmingham farm to Rush for a period of twenty-one years. It was inconceivable that Jermy would agree to such an arrangement, and of course he had not. The documents had been drawn up by Rush, who had coerced Emily Sandford into copying them and then witnessing Jermy's forged signature.

Meantime Mr Isaac Jermy, who during 1847-8 had been living in Great Yarmouth, was not unaware of the machinations of Rush. They had been involved in much litigation which had culminated in March 1848 in an action by Jermy for breach of contracts. An unfavourable result had infuriated Rush, and had impelled him into writing and circulating a scurrilous pamphlet. Space does not permit detailed examination of this document; suffice to say that in it Rush vilified at length Isaac Jermy, insisting that he was wrongfully in possession of the Stanfield estate, and pressing his own claims. It was all couched in grossly inflammatory language, and the wonder is that Jermy did not immediately institute libel proceedings. He maybe decided to treat the matter with contempt, and thus deny his adversary further publicity.

In fact Jermy had already suffered an uncomfortable examination at the hands of the Commissioner when appearing as a witness at Rush's recent bankruptcy hearing, and he had no desire to court further adverse comment.

It is appropriate at this point in the narrative to quote W. Teignmouth Shore, who as editor of *The Trial of J. Blomfield Rush* in the *Notable British Trials* series, explicitly sets out Rush's situation as it stood in November 1848.

(a) Pecuniarily Rush was *in extremis*.

(b) He would shortly have to pay his landlord the mortgage on Potash Farm, etc., a sum which he could not possibly raise.

(c) He possessed documents from Thomas Jermy and John Larner, which if they should succeed in their claim to the Stanfield Hall and Fellingham estates would establish him again in security.

(d) He hated Mr Jermy.

(e) Also, he held the forged agreements between Mr Jermy and himself, which would be valueless unless the former died within a few days.

Tuesday evening, 28 November 1848, was particularly dark and miserable. A bitingly cold north-easterly wind cut through any soul brave enough to venture forth, while occasional rain squalls fell from low-lying clouds that completely obscured the moon.

In Stanfield Hall, near Wymondham, Norfolk, Isaac Jermy had just finished dinner; his son Isaac junior and his wife Sophie had shared his table and had retired to the drawing-room where they were about to commence a game of cards.

Elsewhere in the Hall was Isaac senior's fourteen-year-old daughter Isabella, Watson the butler who was in his pantry, and in the servants' hall the cook, Martha Read, and Eliza Chastney, a housemaid.

The elder Mr Jermy decided to stroll as far as the front porch for a breath of fresh air after his meal. As he reached the door and opened it he was greeted by a swirling of autumn leaves as they gusted into the hall; it was certainly a filthy night. Suddenly he glimpsed a figure emerging out of the blackness; a familiar figure, but now dressed in a cloak with something covering his face. He sensed, rather than saw, the long-barrelled pistol levelled at his chest, and then instant oblivion descended upon him as from point-blank range a shot smashed through the fourth, fifth and sixth ribs before tearing his heart away and lodging its eviscerated remains in the muscular part of his back.

The cloaked and disguised figure, short, thick-set and menacing, ran to the Hall's side door a few yards away and entered the servants' area. He brushed past Watson, who had emerged from his pantry on hearing the explosion, and who hastily returned to the comparative safety of his sanctum upon seeing the cloaked figure with a pistol in his hand. From there the butler watched horror-struck as the assassin came face to face with Mr Jermy junior, hurrying from the lobby to the hall to investigate the commotion. Without hesitation the intruder shot him, again at point-blank range and with the same chilling result as before.

By now the Hall was in an uproar; Sophie Jermy had emerged from the drawing-room, through the hall and into the lobby where she was now screaming hysterically at the sight of her mortally wounded husband. She was being comforted by the housemaid, Eliza Chastney, while Martha Read, the cook, and fourteen-year-old Isabella Jermy were making good their escape from the servants' hall out to the stable.

The shooting was not over. As the assassin returned from the dining-room, across the hall and into the lobby, he was confronted by Sophie Jermy and Eliza Chastney cowering together against the opposite wall. Without hesitation he again raised his pistol and fired, hitting both women this time fortunately without fatal result, Sophie being wounded in the arm and Eliza Chastney in the leg.

After the women had fallen to the ground, the intruder hurried from the Hall by the door by which he had entered, and disappeared into the darkness.

He had left behind a scene of carnage; Isaac Jermy and his son lay dead, Mrs Sophie Jermy and the housemaid were wounded, and the remaining staff were in varying degrees of shock. One of them had reached the Hall bell, which now added to the commotion by tolling its urgent message of distress across the surrounding countryside. Martha Read and young Isabella emerged cautiously from the stable and made their way to the Lodge, as Watson the butler stumbled across the fields to a neighbouring farm to summon help.

A telegraphic message was sent informing the police at Norwich of what had occurred, and suggesting that Rush was the culprit. This information was relayed to other police stations countrywide, but Rush was only a mile away from Stanfield Hall, having returned immediately to Potash Farm.

In the meantime order was gradually being restored at the Hall. Mr Cann, a magistrate from Wymondham arrived, followed by Mr Nichols the family surgeon, who removed several pieces of lead shot from the bodies of both Mr Jermys, who had been laid out on the drawing-room floor. One of the local farmers or gentry who arrived on the scene recovered a piece of paper lying on the hall floor. It had been deliberately dropped by Rush in a crude attempt to cast suspicion on old Thomas Jermy, with whom not long before he had entered into an agreement over Stanfield Hall. The note read,

'There are seven of us here, three of us outside, and four inside the hall, all armed as you see us two. If any of you servants offer to leave the premises or to follow, you will be shot dead. Therefore, all of you keep in the servants' hall, and you nor anyone else will take any harm, for we only come to take of the Stanfield Hall property.' – Thomas Jermy, the owner.

This missive was later produced at the trial.

Shortly after one o'clock in the morning a dozen or more armed policemen arrived from Norwich. After speaking to servants and other occupants of the Hall they moved off into the night and deployed themselves around Potash Farm. After a time a live-in labourer named Savoury was waylaid by the constables as he emerged from the farmhouse to start work, and was instructed to go back and tell his employer that he was wanted downstairs. In due course Rush appeared and was immediately arrested. Before he was taken to the Bridewell at Wymondham for temporary detention, a bewildered Emily Sandford prepared breakfast for him which he ate whilst handcuffed. Emily was soon to learn what had happened during the night at Stanfield Hall, when she was questioned by the police.

During the next four months in custody at Norwich Castle gaol, Rush had ample opportunity to consider his situation. At an inquest into the deaths held at the King's Head, Wymondham in

December, the jury had returned a verdict of wilful murder against him. The verdict did nothing to lessen his determination to conduct his own defence when eventually he stood trial. Nonetheless efforts were still made to persuade Rush to employ counsel, but to no avail; he was the most egocentric of men, convinced of his advocatory ability and having the not entirely misplaced conviction that others would fail to understand the complexities of the case as well as he did himself.

From the time of his arrival at the Castle, until he left it for the last time, Rush professed himself to be a devout man. He made immediate call upon the chaplain, the Reverend Brown, to whom he henceforth incessantly protested his innocence. He pored over his Bible, and regularly attended chapel services. Other members of the prison staff regarded him as a truculent, manipulative inmate.

After Rush's death a letter was found addressed to, but never sent to, his solicitors. In it he described how a few days before the murders he had been approached by a man calling himself Joe, who was accompanied by another man he knew as 'the Lawyer' and a third named Dick. According to Rush they had tried to enlist his help in a forthcoming attempt to seize Stanfield Hall. He had refused, but on the night of 28 November, when the attempt was supposedly to be made, he had gone to the edge of his land and heard gunshots coming from the direction of the Hall. He had immediately hastened back to his farm. This letter tied in neatly with the note he had left at the Hall, and was the line of defence he was to pursue at his trial.

Meanwhile, the prosecution had been preparing its case. They had four principal witnesses – Watson the butler, Eliza Chastney the housemaid and Martha Read the cook, all eye-witnesses of what had taken place, and Emily Sandford, who could testify as to Rush's activities during the two years she had known him.

On 14 December 1848, Rush was committed for trial by the examining magistrates, and on Thursday, 29 March 1849, he stood in the dock at the Spring Assizes at Norwich and pleaded not guilty to murdering Mr Isaac Jermy and his son.

The trial lasted for six days and was presided over by Robert Monsey Rolph (Baron Rolfe of Cranworth), a former Solicitor-General, Baron of Exchequer and Privy Counsellor. At the time of Rush's trial he was fifty-eight years old. He became Lord Chancellor four years later, an office he was to hold for thirteen years.

Presenting the Crown case was John Barnard Byles (Mr Serjeant

Byles), a leading counsel of his day who was also Recorder of Buckingham. Knighted ten years later, his career was to continue until 1873, eleven years before his death. His junior counsel at the trial were Mr Prendergast and Mr Evans. Rush, as has been pointed out, was unrepresented.

Serjeant Byles' opening statement set out clearly and at length the circumstances leading up to the murders at Stanfield Hall. He detailed Rush's machinations in attempting to protect his interests on the estate farms he worked, and in pursuit of the claims to the estate made by old Thomas Jermy and the Larners. He also mentioned the arrival in 1846 of Emily Sandford, and her subsequent unhappy involvement in Rush's scheming. Serjeant Byles ended his speech by describing the events that had taken place on the evening of Tuesday, 28 November 1848, at Stanfield Hall.

As the prosecution prepared to call its witnesses Rush made the first of the frequent interruptions he was to make, by asking that a solicitor, John Stevenson Cann, be called first. His request was acceded to, whereupon Mr Cann testified to a number of letters and documents that he had found secreted by Rush in a closet at Potash Farm, and others he had discovered at Felmingham Farm.

Rush's cross-examination was tedious and often irrelevant, as might have been expected from one unversed in advocacy. Baron Rolfe intervened, as he was obliged to do throughout the trial, to point out that, 'There may be no end to enquiries such as these. A great deal of this is evidence that could not be admitted if you had employed counsel, but I do not wish to be strict with you.' After pausing to listen to the judge, Rush continued unabashed.

There followed the evidence of Watson, Chastney and Read. All recounted the events on the night of the murders. Chastney was carried into court lying on a makeshift stretcher, not yet recovered from her injuries. Like the other two, she told of seeing a man in the hall brandishing a gun or pistol. Although the man's face was masked, she had formed a definite impression as to his identity. 'Who do you believe it to be?' asked Mr Prendergast. 'The prisoner,' she replied.

Watson was equally certain. After telling the court in considerable detail of what had taken place, including the fact that the man had passed within three feet of him and had dropped two pieces of paper in the passageway, he was asked by Serjeant Byles, 'Who was that man?' and he replied,

'I believe that man was the prisoner Rush.'

Finally Martha Read, the cook. Although preoccupied in looking after Isabella Jermy, who had run into the servants' hall crying, 'Oh! Read, we shall all be murdered,' she had nonetheless had a good sighting of the man before her, and her young charge had escaped to the stable. She described him to Mr Evans, 'He was a low, stout man. I have repeatedly seen Rush at the Hall. The man was of the height, size, and carriage of Rush, and as soon as I saw him my impression was that it was Rush, and that is my impression still.' Against such unequivocal testimony from the three servants, Rush made very little impression during his cross-examination.

The remainder of the first day was given over to the evidence of the two surgeons, Messrs Nichols and Tunaley, who had each examined the bodies at Stanfield Hall on the night of the shooting. They told of the injuries to the deceased, and mentioned also that Sophie Jermy's arm had since been amputated. Both described removing pieces of lead from the bodies, and from the leg of Eliza Chastney.

The testimony and cross-examination of Emily Sandford occupied the entire second day, and the greater part of the third day of the trial. She stood in the witness box, a lone, forlorn figure, wearing her Sunday-best clothes, aware that as the mistress of the accused she excited little sympathy from those in court. Gradually however, feelings towards her changed, as after telling of her life with Rush, she tried to answer the questions he put in cross-examination.

Mr Prendergast led Emily through the events that had taken place since she had first met Rush two years before and had gone to live at Stanfield Hall Farm. How in February, 1848, she had moved to Islington where a meeting had taken place between Rush, Thomas Jermy, Larner and a man called Read. These last three had signed a document that had been copied by her at Rush's bidding from one he himself had written. Emily explained that she had later moved to Potash Farm, and had subsequently taken lodgings in Norwich. It was while she was there, she said, that Rush had brought her some more documents to copy, and later to witness. When she demurred at signing these papers, Rush became angry with her. She then told Mr Prendergast that at the beginning of November, 1848 she returned to Potash Farm, where Rush again coerced her into witnessing other documents he had prepared.

Emily went on to describe the events of 28 November. Of how she had been looking forward to accompanying Rush in the evening to a concert in Norwich, but that at the last minute he had called it off, saying that he was unwell. Despite this he had gone out at half-past-seven, and upon returning at nine or half-past, 'He looked pale, ill and agitated ... I asked him what was the matter, and if anything had happened. He replied, "No nothing; if you hear any enquiries for me, say I was out only ten minutes." '

Rush's cross-examination dwelt at length on irrelevancies; the clothes she had been wearing on the 28th; the seat he had been occupying in the parlour; his own conduct since they had known each other, and the fact that they had agreed to 'cease all connection with each other ... so that one might not have a house full of children', to which remark Emily was stung into replying, 'I don't know why you wish to insult me, sir.'

He asked her how long they had sat over their tea that evening, and the length of time she estimated he had been absent. She answered him as best she could, but she constantly reminded him that as she had not been wearing her watch, and there was no clock in the parlour, she was unable to quote exact times. At this Rush became heated, 'I will ask you if I did not tell you to look at your watch – try and recollect – be composed for God's sake,' he entreated her.

'No, certainly you did not. I should recollect if you had,' replied Emily.

'For God's sake recollect,' insisted Rush.

'No, you did not. I cannot recollect any such thing,' Emily repeated.

And so it continued for the rest of Friday and into the Saturday. Baron Rolfe, invariably courteous, and ever mindful that Rush was unrepresented, could not prevent his impatience showing occasionally. 'What has this to do with this charge?' he asked, when Rush referred to an old will of Mr Jermy's father. On another occasion, when Rush was questioning Emily about letters that had passed between them, he warned him, 'If you ask questions like these I must confine you within certain limits. There is not a third part of all that has been stated which is connected with the real question at issue.'

'My lord, look here,' Rush started, but the judge's patience was all but exhausted; 'I cannot allow you to proceed,' he said.

Nevertheless Rush did proceed; remonstrating one minute, cajoling the next, his remaining cross-examination of Emily Sandford bearing little relevance to the testimony she had given the previous day. At last it ended, and with it died his two year relationship with Emily.

If those in court thought that they had withstood the worst of Rush's loquaciousness, they were in for a shock when later he stood up to speak in his own defence.

Meanwhile the remaining prosecution witnesses were called. The rest of the third day was taken up by a miscellany of witnesses, including a servant girl from the Hall who had been in the grounds with friends when she had heard gunfire, and who had later picked up the second piece of paper dropped by Rush in the passageway. A former clerk of Rush's from the days when he had been working as an auctioneer and valuer, and an acquaintance of Mr Jermy both stated that the documents earlier produced were in the accused's handwriting, but that the signatures, purporting to be those of Isaac Jermy, were not his.

Another witness on the Saturday, William Howe, told the court of how in his presence Rush had exhibited overt animosity towards Isaac Jermy. Rush cross-examined Howe at length in an unsuccessful attempt to discredit him.

The final prosecution witnesses called on Monday, were the policemen who had been present at Rush's arrest. One of these, George Pont, described how with other officers he had gone first to Stanfield Hall where he had seen the bodies of Mr Jermy and his son. They had then continued on to Potash Farm and kept watch until Savoury had appeared and had been instructed to go and tell Rush that he was wanted. Pont had then arrested him as soon as he came down to the kitchen. 'I said, "You must consider yourself my prisoner, on suspicion of murdering the two Mr Jermys last night". I handcuffed him at the same time. He first said, "The two Mr Jermys murdered! I don't like these", alluding to the handcuffs. "God knows I am clear of that".' Pont had then gone upstairs to Rush's bedroom, where in a closet he had discovered two double-barrelled guns. He later escorted Rush to the Bridewell at Wymondham.

Other officers followed Pont and largely corroborated what he had said. One of them, Thomas Osborn, told of remarks made by Rush to Emily Sandford before he left for the Bridewell: ' "I am accused of murdering Jermy and his son ... but you and Savoury can clear me ... " Rush asked her if she had been questioned, to which she replied, "I said you went out at eight o'clock for about a quarter of an hour". He said, "I was not more than ten minutes".'

Emily's loyalty had been strained to the utmost, as by then she knew of the murders, and knowing also of Rush's absence from the farm the previous evening she almost certainly suspected him of some involvement. She was a devout young woman, and although under his influence she undoubtedly still had some affection for him. This was only to disappear entirely when later she learnt the full extent of his deception.

Rush's aggressive cross-examination of the police witnesses had little effect apart from eliciting details that from his point of view would have been best left unsaid.

On the morning of Tuesday, 3 April 1849, the fifth day of his trial, the squat figure of Rush, soberly dressed in black, stepped from the dock to the witness box to present his defence. His own speech would not end until noon the following day, by which time he would have been speaking for almost fourteen hours.

Its length precludes adequate paraphrasing in a short account, so I will try to convey its general tenor, and attempt to extract some of the more important points from a mass of irrelevancies.

The inherent disadvantage in being unrepresented soon became apparent during Rush's exhortation. He continually invoked divine intercession – 'God Almighty' would protect him, 'God Almighty' knew he was innocent – and frequently appealed to the jury to think of his 'dear little children' when considering his submissions.

Early on he introduced the story of Joe, 'the Lawyer' and Dick, and in the same breath he referred to the lies that he alleged had been told by Emily Sandford and other witnesses. He frequently merged his arguments and submissions, making it even more difficult for those listening to comprehend them.

In one respect he remained consistent – his utter repudiation of Emily Sandford's evidence. He constantly alluded to her testimony and the lies he said it contained, 'This was my especial desire in my cross-examination of that person,' referring to Emily. 'I tried to elicit the truth ...' he said. 'If what Sandford had to state was the truth, what had she to suffer? Could he have ever believed she would have come forward and stated what she did? She must have had a bad character. ... The evidence given before the coroner and the magistrates would show that the statement she made then was completely at variance with her present one ...' and so he went on.

Rush spoke disparagingly of the evidence of the three eye-witnesses: James Watson: his evidence 'amounted to little';

Eliza Chastney: ' ...hers was the most extraordinary evidence ever given'; and Martha Read: 'never had a woman given evidence with a worse motive and a more hostile spirit than she had done'. Baron Rolfe interrupted to observe drily, 'I suppose the meaning you wish to convey to the jury is that no evidence exists to show the man came out' (from the hall into the passageway).

'Just so,' replied Rush.

Police Constable Pont's evidence also came under attack from Rush. 'The barefacedness of Pont was most infamous.' He tried unsuccessfully to play-off the evidence of one policeman against another.

So it went on for a day-and-a-half. Allegations, refutations, tantrums, tears, maudlin sentimentality, aggressiveness – the court were treated to the whole gamut of his emotions.

Rush called only five witnesses. The sum total of their evidence did little to help his case. A solicitor, George Waugh, said that he had had brief contact with him before his trial, and had recommended that he should not defend himself. Another witness, Arthur Walker Hyde, was called to discredit an earlier witness named William Howe. Hyde stated that he had met Howe in a coffee shop and that during their conversation the latter had said that he would attend the trial and swear either way for £20. Howe was first called to deny this, and then under cross-examination by Serjeant Byles, Hyde's own credentials and reliability as a witness were called into question.

Rush's labourer Savoury swore that he had last seen his employer at Potash Farm on the evening of the murder at between seven and seven-thirty, and definitely not as late as eight o'clock. He would have been of more value to the prosecution.

Finally, Marie Blanchflower, a nurse at Stanfield Hall, stated that she saw the intruder on the night of the murders, but did not identify him as Rush. However, her testimony that she saw 'a low, stout man, broad shoulders, no hat on', and that she brushed by him, was negated when Rush asked her, 'Did you pass me quickly?' a calamitous slip of the tongue if correctly reported.

At Rush's request two provocative letters he had written to Isaac Jermy senior in April, 1848, were tendered in evidence, but Baron Rolfe refused him permission to read out part of the defamatory pamphlet he had circulated. Rush at last sat down, complaining to the end that he had not been allowed to present all the documentary evidence, or call all the witnesses he desired.

At the beginning of his own closing speech, Serjeant Byles pointed out that 'certainly the present trial has exceeded in the annals of judicial long-suffering anything that was ever before experienced'.

Rush had certainly been allowed far more latitude than would have been the case had he been represented. In contrast Serjeant Byles' closing remarks were confined to the evidence that had been given over the previous four-and-a-half days. He recapitulated the testimony of Watson, Chastney and Read, maintained that Rush himself was the author of the notes found in the hall on the night of 28 November, and commented sympathetically on Emily Sandford's involvement, testimony and cross-examination. 'That young person has made the only atonement she could make ... you have heard her cross-examined at a length to which, never in all my experience, did I hear any witness, either male or female, be examined. She was in that box thirteen hours, of which nine or ten were occupied in her cross-examination.'

Serjeant Byles went on to describe Rush's behaviour on the night of the murders. His indisposition at teatime that had aroused Emily's suspicion; his departure at about half-past-seven and return after two hours to disappear into his room from where he re-emerged later in a nervous, agitated state.

The prosecutor reminded the court of how, whilst out earlier the same day, he had received confirmation that both Mr Jermys were at home from a woman of whom he had enquired. The route between Potash Farm and Stanfield Hall was carefully retraced by Serjeant Byles, who drew the jury's attention to the fact that the boots Rush had worn that night had never been found, thus preventing any comparison with footmarks he may have left. Why had Rush not mentioned the three men, Joe, Dick and 'the Lawyer', at the magistrates' hearing, asked Serjeant Byles. Here Rush interrupted, 'I had no business to do it. I had no business to accuse others ...'

Before ending, the prosecuting advocate referred again briefly to the forged documents: 'Thomas Jermy had been placed in the box. He can't write; therefore he could not have written the paper.' He then alluded to the unhappy relationship that existed between Rush and the Jermys, father and son, 'the bad feeling shown by the prisoner towards Mr Jermy and his son ... I grieve to say the prisoner had no property, as he was about to be turned out of the farm', and went on to the question of motive, ' ... I think the jury will not find it difficult to discover a motive for the crime charged against the prisoner.' As Serjeant Byles sat down, Rush may have felt that his infallibility had been dented after all.

There remained only Baron Rolfe's summing up. The evidence that had been heard was gone over once again; the judge dismissed the hypothesis that the two Jermys had been shot by different individuals, pointing out that the remains of the lead shot removed from the bodies were 'exactly alike', thus proving that one man had shot them both. After referring to the eye-witness testimony, he moved on to the circumstantial evidence – the fact that after being at the farm all day, the accused had gone out at the material time, to return later in a state of some agitation. He recalled Emily Sandford's testimony and cross-examination as to the events of that Tuesday night; of how Rush had gone to her room and discussed with her, among other things, the concert in Norwich that they had missed. However, they seemed to have avoided talking about events that had taken place elsewhere during Rush's absence.

The judge referred to the supposed involvement of Thomas Jermy, Larner and others, and to Rush's testimony that after hearing shots fired and the Hall bell tolling when out that night, he had hastened back to the farm. Why, asked Baron Rolfe, had he not mentioned this to the magistrates before whom he had appeared the following morning, instead of leaving it until his trial? The judge concluded by referring briefly to the transactions involving the forged documents, and to Emily Sandford's involvement in the compiling of those documents.

For almost six days those in court had listened to a total of forty-four witnesses, apart from the accused, who alone had spoken for the best part of a day-and-a-half. It must therefore have been a stupendous anticlimax when the jury filed back into court after just ten minutes absence to announce that they had found the prisoner guilty. Rush, on hearing this, burst out typically, 'My Lord, I am innocent of that, thank God Almighty.'

Baron Rolfe prefaced the death sentence with an overlong tirade; at one point he told Rush that had he kept his promise to marry Emily Sandford, she may well have invoked her legal right, and refused to testify against him. Rush could not resist commenting, 'I did not make any promise.' Otherwise he remained silent as the judge told him that, 'You must quit this world by an ignominious death,' whilst twice reminding him that his conduct whilst still on earth was a matter of 'indifference' to society. Eventually sentence was pronounced, allowing him to depart from the stage he had dominated for the previous six days.

Rush was returned to Norwich Castle to await his execution. He continued to maintain his innocence, despite the overwhelming weight of evidence against him. He steadfastly refused to confess or repent, and in fact on the morning of his execution he became exceedingly irritated with both the prison chaplain and the Reverend Andrew, the Ketteringham minister, each of whom tried vainly to urge this course upon him.

The weather was grey and dismal as between twelve and thirteen thousand spectators assembled before the Castle on Saturday, 21 April 1849, to witness the final drama. Rush, still dressed entirely in black, emerged and walked unaided to the scaffold erected outside the main entrance. As if in a final gesture of defiance, he turned away from the crowd to face the castle walls as the white hood was placed over his head.

Seconds later the hush that had come over the crowd was broken as the trap doors crashed open, and in the words of the Reverend Andrew ' ... like a bird in a storm that cannot fly, he was carried away as with a whirlwind, suddenly, violently and irresistibly'.

Rush was rightly convicted of the murders at Stanfield Hall, of that I am convinced. Rarely has murder been so flagrantly committed before witnesses, many of whom were familiar enough with the perpetrator as to be able to identify him despite his disguise.

Rush was not mad in the legal sense – he knew what he was doing, and what he was doing he knew was wrong. He almost certainly held the view that his acts were justified, and was motivated above all else by his pathological hatred of Mr Isaac Jermy senior, a hatred that extended, when the time came, to other members of his family and household.

Rush's malignancy towards the Jermy family was born out of resentment. Prior to Isaac Jermy succeeding to the estate in 1837, Rush had been on amicable terms with his father, from whom he leased Felmingham and Stanfield Hall farms on very favourable terms. This changed drastically when the younger Mr Jermy took over the estate, and resulted in the ensuing emnity. By 1848, Rush's financial situation was desperate, and this precipitated the events of 28 November. After having committed the crime, discovery was inevitable, and indeed within a few hours he had been arrested.

I believe that Rush was indifferent to the consequences of his acts that night. He was not unintelligent, his experience as an auctioneer and valuer indicate otherwise. Therefore his futile efforts to cast suspicion elsewhere, his grotesque disguise and the belated introduction of Joe, 'the Lawyer' and Dick, I cannot believe were serious attempts by him to avoid detection and its consequences. Instead I consider that after killing the Jermys he felt that justice had been served and his mission accomplished. The wounding of Sophie Jermy and Eliza Chastney in my view was a compulsive act committed impetuously as he was confronted by the two women in the hallway. His decision to defend himself, and his subsequent conduct during his trial – particularly the prolonged cross-examination of Emily Sandford, and his own interminable, and at times irrational speech – illustrate his desire to portray Jermy in the worst possible light, and himself as his long-suffering victim.

Unfortunately for Rush the course of the trial did not go as he had anticipated; a comparatively short time was devoted to the disputes leading up to the crime, whilst much longer was spent in hearing of the circumstances and subsequent events surrounding the murders. As a result, James Blomfield Rush is best remembered as the pitiless, vengeful killer of two defenceless victims at Stanfield Hall.

# 10   A Beauty Spot Shooting, Cambridgeshire 1976

Life! As Peter Littlechild stepped out of sight from the dock at Norwich Crown Court on 5 May 1976, to begin a life sentence, he may well have reflected on the ill-fated breakdown of his car one morning four months before. If that hadn't happened his victim would probably still be alive, and he would be going about his day-to-day business as usual, instead of being a convicted murderer.

The sound of shots coming from Byron's Pool, a local beauty spot off the Grantchester to Trumpington road near Cambridge, excited only slight curiosity on the morning of Tuesday, 6 January 1976. That is with the exception of William Sweet, a fifty-year-old family man who had gone to the pool early that morning for a day's fishing. Besides angling, Sweet was a keen naturalist who was strongly averse to blood sports. This Tuesday morning Sweet had with him his camera, hoping to snap some wildlife photographs.

This much is known: what followed can only be assumed from evidence that emerged at the subsequent trial.

Peter Littlechild, a twenty-four-year-old cavity wall insulator, had set out that day from his home in Cambridge to go to work at Wittering near Huntingdon. Exasperated when his car engine malfunctioned, he had decided to return home. It had then occurred to him to stop off at Byron's Pool to do some shooting. A keen marksman, he had with him his twelve-bore, illegally sawn-off shot-gun. It would be the second day in a row that he had been to the pool, as a change from target shooting at home with his air gun.

It didn't take Littlechild long to reach the pool, and soon after entering the surrounding woods he spotted a pheasant. Quickly he raised his gun and fired.

What followed is not clear; it seems that very soon afterwards Sweet appeared on the scene in a state of some agitation at having heard the sound of the detonation. He probably became even more incensed at the sight of the dead pheasant, and it seems likely that a violent altercation ensued.

Littlechild later described to the police what he alleged had happened: 'I ... was just shooting at small birds and tree stumps. I was sort of minding my own business. I was facing the river. Next thing I knew this fellow was ranting and raving and running at me. I didn't even know what he was saying. It [the gun] went bang.' This statement was quite possibly true as far as it went – there is certainly no suggestion that Littlechild had gone to Byron's Pool to seek out William Sweet and shoot him. It is probable also that he was taken aback at the unexpected verbal onslaught directed at him by the other man. However it is most unlikely that the 'ranting and raving' was entirely one-sided, and although undoubtedly the gun went bang, Littlechild omitted to mention that this was when Sweet was between twenty and fifty feet away and had his back to him, or as the prosecution later alleged was, 'very probably running away'.

Forensic and ballistic experts later testified that three shots were fired at Sweet: the first two, into his back and leg, were non-fatal, although they no doubt slowed him down as he tried to flee. The third and final shot was fired from very close range, expert opinion later giving the distance as between point-blank and six feet. This blast hit Sweet full in the side of the face and head with devastating and instantaneous results. Before firing this last shot Littlechild would had to have reloaded, thus negating his later assertion that the shooting was accidental.

Littlechild had stared in disbelief at the man lying on the ground before him with half his face and head missing. He stood momentarily paralysed, appalled at what had taken place. Suddenly he became aware of his own situation, so grabbing hold of the dead man's feet he dragged him along the path for a few yards before depositing him in the abundant undergrowth. After concealing the body as best he could, Littlechild had run to his car and driven from the scene. Soon afterwards he stopped at the bridge crossing the River Ouse at Stretham and dropped his shot-gun and the remaining cartridges into the water below.

Another fisherman had intended making an early start at Byron's Pool that Tuesday. Neil Everard, a policeman from

Saffron Walden, had also been there the day before and had noticed both the parked car and the dark-haired, bearded man in the woods by the pool. Both the car and the man later disappeared, but now on the following day he was to remember both.

Everard overslept that Tuesday morning and so arrived much later than he had intended. After parking his car and gathering together fishing tackle, he picked his way along the path towards his favourite spot at the pool's edge. As he trekked forward he saw what appeared to be a wellington boot protruding from the undergrowth. He paid it little attention until, upon reaching the pool, he noticed a fishing-rod on its rest, a bait box and other fisherman's paraphernalia, and a camera lying in the mud at the pool's edge. Of the owner there was no sign.

Everard felt uneasy, and remembering the wellington boot he had seen, he retraced his steps to investigate it further. Pushing aside the undergrowth and leaves, the lifeless body of William Sweet met his gaze. A trail of blood led from what remained of his head along the path to a larger pool a few yards further on.

It was a week during which the knighthood bestowed on Richard Attenborough, the retirement of the former British, Commonwealth and European heavyweight boxing champion, Joe Bugner, and the slaughter in a small south Armagh village of ten Protestant workmen dominated the headlines. Locally in Cambridge these events were for a time overshadowed by news of the discovery of a body at Byron's Pool, and of the police hunt that followed.

Within minutes of hearing of the finding of the body, Detective Chief Superintendent Charles Naan, the Cambridge CID chief, was on his way with other officers from police headquarters to the scene. They were soon followed by several dozen of their uniformed colleagues who arrived with their equipment to carry out a painstaking search of the pool and its environs. Whilst police frogmen dived to the bottom of the murky waters to search for the murder weapon, other officers, assisted by handlers and their dogs, combed the woods and undergrowth. Elsewhere detectives interviewed and took statements from people who had heard the shots, seen cars parked in the vicinity or could help with other information.

By the evening of that first day investigators in the incident room at Cambridge police station were busily analysing the information being disseminated from the mobile communications caravan at the scene. The searchers had found the packing wads from several spent twelve bore cartridges, but had still not traced the gun. The next day Royal Engineers equipped with mine detectors would arrive to help with the search.

Meanwhile the police, having soon established the victim's identity from items found at or near the murder scene, learnt more of his background. They confirmed that apart from his passionate opposition to blood sports – he was a member of the League Against Cruel Sports – there was nothing to single out William Sweet from millions of other family men.

Happily married with two grown-up daughters, he had for many years been a greengrocer, and both he and his wife Stella were well known to many Cambridge housewives. Twelve months before his death a heart condition had persuaded him to give up his business, and in January, 1976, he was working as a porter at Girton College. His outdoor interests revolved around fishing, and he was a respected and active member of several local angling clubs.

What was it, wondered Naan, that had induced someone to kill a popular, hard-working family man, whose only apparent deviation from normality was his strong opposition to blood sports, a feeling shared in any case by very many of his fellow countrymen. Naan was determined to find the answer to that question, and with it the identity of the person who had squeezed the trigger.

The arrest of a suspect for the murder was not long delayed; intensive police activity and enquiries, led and co-ordinated by Naan and his deputy, Detective Superintendent Keith Hookham, had resulted in a wealth of information. In addition there was PC Everard, who had not only seen the suspect's car, but the man himself on the Monday.

As there were not that many men living in and around Cambridge with firearms convictions, it was not too difficult a task to eliminate them as possible suspects until one remained who fitted the description provided by PC Everard. Peter David Littlechild, a twenty-four-year-old married man living off Histon Road in Cambridge, had appeared at Wisbech Crown Court the previous July and had been given a twelve month suspended sentence for unlawfully possessing a firearm and ammunition. After verifying that he owned a motor car similar to that seen near the pool, Naan decided that it would be worth bringing him to police headquarters for questioning.

Thus on the evening of Wednesday, 7 January, barely thirty-six hours since the shooting had occurred, a police car drew up outside Littlechild's address.

David Littlechild had been dreading the police visit. Ever since fleeing from Byron's Pool the previous morning, he had known that sooner or later they would want to see him about the shooting. He was no stranger to the local constabulary, and since his appearance at Wisbech he had suspected that they had been keeping a wary eye upon him. Nevertheless the knock announcing the police arrival was still a shock when it came. Exactly a week before it had been New Year's Eve: 1976 had soon turned sour, he thought.

Littlechild knew some of the detectives who had come for him. Before leaving the house they asked a few innocuous questions about his movements the previous day, but he knew that the serious questioning would come later at the station, out of his family's hearing. As he was driven away his wife watched and wondered how long it would be before her husband stepped through their front door again.

Later that night Detective Chief Superintendent Naan issued a short communiqué to the press starting with the time-worn police euphemism for a suspect being under arrest, 'A man is helping us with our enquiries in connection with our murder investigation at Grantchester. He will remain here at police headquarters overnight. The question of charges is still to be considered ...'

Littlechild had been helping the police, although extracting the truth from him had not been easy. At first he had denied any involvement in the murder, telling Naan and Hookham that he had been at home. In a second statement he admitted having been at Byron's Pool on the Monday and Tuesday, but said that he had been sitting in his car eating his sandwiches at the material time. 'I heard some bangs – I thought they were from the rifle range at Barton Road,' he had told his questioners.

Naan and Hookham were still not satisfied, and continued with their questioning. Quite suddenly Littlechild seemed to accept the hopelessness of his situation. He asked first to telephone his wife, and then turning to Naan, in reply to the policeman's question as to why the shooting had happened, the words poured out with no regard for sequence, 'I was frightened. I can tell you where the gun is. It is in the river by Stretham Bridge. It's all at Stretham.'

Naan asked him what he meant by 'all' and Littlechild told him, 'His watch came off while I was dragging him. He was coming at me. I fired at him.'

'Did you shoot him in the face?' asked the detective.

'I shot him on the side of the head I think.'

'How did you manage to shoot him twice in the back?' Littlechild, realizing the significance of the question hesitated and didn't answer directly, 'I should have my solicitor, don't you think?'

The policemen had no objections; they knew that they had William Sweet's killer, and were quite prepared to accede to his legitimate requests. When Littlechild later made a third statement recounting in more detail what had happened, his solicitor David Tucker was present.

Earlier Mrs Littlechild had arrived at the police station anxious to find out more about her husband's arrest. She had already told the police that he owned an airgun, but the conversation they had at the station indicated that she was unaware of the shot-gun. After he had tried first to reassure her, she asked him,

'Did you do it?'

'Yes,' he replied.

'Why?'

'Who knows why? That's one question I can't answer,' her husband replied.

'Where did you get the gun?' she next asked.

'I have had it for a long time,' he answered evasively.

The next morning the police went to the spot indicated by Littlechild and retrieved from the waters of Wicken Fen his shot-gun, cartridges (one of them used), and items of personal property that had belonged to William Sweet. Naan and his team were satisfied; with the finding of the gun, the chain of evidence was complete. The following morning, Friday, Littlechild made a brief appearance before the Cambridge magistrates charged with William Sweet's murder.

In May 1976 a new car cost £2000, a job as an egg collector for Sainsbury's paid £28 for a forty-hour week and Liverpool clinched the League Championship for a record ninth time after a 3-1 away win against Wolverhampton Wanderers.

More seriously, four Irishmen appeared in court in London charged in connection with the Balcombe Street siege, while the Jeremy Thorpe scandal attracted the avid attention of the media.

It is doubtful if any of this was of much interest to Peter Littlechild, for on the third of the month his trial had commenced at Norwich Crown Court. He stood in the dock that first morning, dark-haired and bearded, a stocky figure casually dressed in an open-necked shirt and pullover, and pleaded not guilty to the murder indictment. He was represented by John Marriage QC (see also Chapter 5), while the Crown case was presented by Mr William Howard, QC. Mr Justice Stocker was the presiding judge.

Mr Howard opened the Crown case by describing the prosecution version of what had occurred on Tuesday, 6 January. Of how Sweet had gone fishing at Byron's Pool, only to be shot dead, his body later being found by PC Everard. The jury were shown photographs of the dead man's body while Mr Howard indicated pellet wounds to his back and leg. He emphasized that the weapon must have been reloaded during the shooting.

The prosecutor continued by telling of the police investigation and their interviews with the accused man following his arrest, and of the statement of admission he had finally made. He claimed that whilst in police custody Littlechild had been visited by his brother and had said to him, 'I fired at him. This bloke came running and I fired. It was so quick.'

Mr Howard ended by telling the jury that 'whatever had passed between Mr Sweet and Mr Littlechild, Mr Littlechild had put the gun close to Mr Sweet's head and fired. You cannot put a shotgun within inches of a man's head and then pull the trigger without intending to kill'.

Before any prosecution witnesses were called, Mr Marriage stood up and admitted on behalf of his client that he had *accidentally* fired the shot that had killed William Sweet.

Four witnesses then testified as to having heard gunshots coming from the direction of Byron's Pool. One of them, George Sewell, had heard five shots altogether, with a distinct pause between the second and third.

There was silence in the court room as the pathologist, Professor Geoffrey Austin Gresham (see also Chapters 5 and 7) after first confirming that death had occurred between 8.00 a.m. and 9.00 a.m., went on to describe William Sweet's injuries. There were three separate wounds he said, two superficial ones to the back of his body, and the fatal one which had destroyed half his skull and brain; all were typical shot-gun injuries. After examining the sawn-off shot-gun which was allegedly the murder weapon, the witness agreed that it could have been fired from a range of six feet.

The Professor caused a minor sensation when he told the court that although the deceased had suffered from a heart condition that could have proved fatal at any time, he attributed his death solely to the gunshot wounds.

The pathologist was followed into the witness box by Geoffrey Brunt, a ballistics expert from the Nottingham forensic science laboratory. Brunt stated that after having examined William Sweet's injuries, he had come to the conclusion that those to the back and leg had resulted from shots fired from between seven and fifteen yards away, while the head wound 'could only have been caused when the muzzle of the gun was within inches of the face, if not touching', thus slightly differing from the estimate of Professor Gresham.

The prosecution concluded with the police evidence. This included that of PC Everard, the off-duty officer who had found the body, and two other officers who had been present at the police station when Littlechild had spoken first to his wife, 'It wasn't enough. It didn't satisfy me,' when she had mentioned his target shooting at home with his airgun, and later to his brother, 'I'm not making excuses, because I shot the bloke.'

Finally Detective Chief Superintendent Naan gave evidence of his interview with Littlechild. Of how after first denying the killing, he later admitted it, 'I just could not believe I had done it, then I got panicky ... I am relieved it's all over, I didn't mean to kill him.'

'But could it have been an accident?' asked Mr Howard in his final speech to the jury. 'Three shots were fired from the same gun, so you can exclude an accident because there must have been reloading, and you can't reload a shot-gun accidentally.' Earlier he had told the jury that the evidence forced them to the conclusion that Littlechild was a murderer. The shots first to the back and leg, and finally to the head, 'fits in', said Mr Howard, 'with the picture of a man running away from a man with a gun'.

The defence did not call any witnesses, relying instead upon Mr Marriage's oratorical skill to raise doubt in the jury's mind as to whether the shooting was deliberate or accidental.

A tragic accident was to be the defence's answer to the prosecution's allegations. From the outset it was the only alternative that stood the remotest chance of being accepted. Mr Marriage advanced a credible hypothesis, but in the end the odds were too heavily weighted against him.

'Is it impossible that the defendant should swing round and

discharge the gun in the face of Mr Sweet?' he asked. No, that was possible, is the answer; one could also agree when he said, 'It's not very difficult to envisage the circumstances of the defendant shooting twice without taking care.' Far less easy to explain however, was the third, fatal shot to the head. Littlechild's counsel attempted to account for this by suggesting that he had carelessly discharged both barrels without being aware that he had hit William Sweet, and then having reloaded he fired a third time with fatal results, but again unknowingly. It is difficult to reconcile this with the evidence of the pathologist and ballistics expert, despite Mr Marriage's comment that there was an 'interesting conflict' between them as to the range from which the shots were fired.

The defence counsel also drew attention to the absence of blood on Littlechild's clothing, and tentatively suggested that the testimony of witnesses who had heard the shots did not fit in with the prosecution's 'row between the two men' theory, an apparent reference to the interval between the shots.

Mr Marriage was aware throughout that the main obstacle to his 'accident' theory was the third shot fired after reloading. It was a stumbling-block that in the end proved insuperable, despite his unremitting attempts to convince the jury of its feasibility.

Mr Justice Stocker also made reference to the third shot; during his summing-up he carefully evaluated the evidence that had been brought before the court during the preceding three days. He dwelt particularly upon the expert evidence, and also spent some time appraising the lengthy interviews Littlechild had had with the police and the subsequent statements he had made.

The jury retired to consider the alternatives. Had Littlechild callously shot William Sweet, possibly after a heated argument, or, as the defence maintained, had it been a tragic accident brought about by the criminal negligence of the accused?

Littlechild listened unmoved as the jury foreman announced the guilty verdict. In view of the damning evidence against him, and the statements he had made, the result probably did not surprise him.

In retrospect the tragedy of the Byron's Pool murder, apart from the untimely death of William Sweet, the inoffensive, likeable family man, who could however become passionately aroused in his defence of wildlife, was the unfortunate circumstance that brought the two men together that winter's morning. As they arrived at the pool, neither could have remotely envisaged the events that were to follow. Both were concerned solely with their own respective pursuits. Unfortunately those clashed when Sweet became aware that Littlechild was engaged in shooting his beloved wildlife.

I have speculated from the evidence available on what I believe took place; if I have drawn the right conclusions, it would seem that the ultimate tragedy could still have been averted if Littlechild, in a fit of madness, had not reloaded his gun and fired that fatal third shot.

# 11   PC Gutteridge, Essex 1927

The two men stared at each other; the one, a policeman lying on his back in a fog-shrouded Essex lane, the other standing over him, a .45 calibre Webley service revolver in his hand. 'What are you looking at me like that for?' asked the man with the gun. The policeman, already dying from two bullet wounds in the face, could only stare mutely back, shock and terror reflected in his eyes. Suddenly the other man stooped forward, and with his revolver held no more than six inches from his victim's face, took deliberate aim and shot him once through each eye. He turned back to his companion, and then both men climbed into a blue Morris Cowley and drove rapidly off into the darkness.

Even with the increased violence of the 1980s, the murder of an unarmed policeman still provokes outrage and anger. In 1927 these feelings were even more evident than they are today. Less than ten years had elapsed since the end of the First World War. The 'Twenties', apart from producing the trend-setting 'Flappers', Oxford bags and a succession of frenetic dances, witnessed also growing unemployment, the economic depression, a General Strike and for many, sheer, grinding poverty.

Two developments since 1918 had changed the habits of many post-war criminals; the proliferation of firearms, most of which had survived from the war, and the advent of the motor car.

Handguns, many brought home by ex-servicemen as souvenirs, soon began to find their way into the hands of ruthless, unscrupulous men who would use them without hesitation should the need arise. The motor car brought previously unheard of mobility to such malefactors.

Frederick Guy Browne and William Henry Kennedy were not themselves products of post-war crime, but both were prepared to take advantage of the opportunities they now saw offered.

The two had first met in Dartmoor. Browne, a thirty-six-year-old south Londoner with a formidable record, was the more dominant character. Slightly below average height, powerfully built with piercing eyes and sporting a walrus moustache, there was an innate aggressiveness about him. His hatred of the police and his violent disposition were well known to the officers acquainted with him. Kennedy was a Scotsman, seven years older than Browne. Slightly taller but more sparingly built, his only noticeable feature was his thinning red hair. He could fairly be described as Browne's intellectual superior, but in all other respects he failed to match up to the younger man.

Browne ran a small motor repair business known as the Globe Garage at 7a, Northcote Road, Battersea, only a few hundred yards from where he lived at 33a, Sister Avenue. Since July Kennedy had worked as his manager.

It was from here on the evening of Monday, 26 September 1927, that the two men set out for Essex with the intention of stealing a motor car and returning to London. They travelled by train to Billericay, where Browne's first attempt to steal a vehicle was discouraged by a dog barking. Further on he selected a house belonging to Dr Edward Lovell, a local GP who had left his car, a blue Morris Cowley containing his medical bag, locked in his garage.

The two men waited until the household had retired before forcing the garage door. They then pushed the car 100 yards down the road, started it and drove away.

Browne's intended route back to London avoided main roads as far as possible. He drove for several miles along country lanes and through darkened villages before arriving with his companion on the Romford to Ongar road. Suddenly a lamp flashed in the darkness ahead, but Browne ignored it and continued past. Almost immediately the sound of a policeman's whistle penetrated above the sound of the engine, so in response he pulled into the side of the road, hitting the bank as he did so. Both men sat waiting until seconds later the figure of Police Constable Gutteridge appeared out of the darkness.

Thirty-eight-year-old George Gutteridge had been a policeman for seventeen years. Suffolk born, he had joined the Essex force in 1910 and since then, apart from a year in the army, he had been stationed in the south of the county before being posted to the village of Stapleford Abbots in 1922. He had married in 1913, and at the time of his death he and his wife Rose had two children,

Muriel, aged twelve years and a four-year-old son named Jackie.

The bluff, genial country policeman was a capable officer who knew how to take care of himself. As one of his colleagues said later, 'I had known PC Gutteridge through the whole of his seventeen years service, and I know that had he been given half a chance he would have rendered a good account of himself that night.' Tragically, George Gutteridge was not given even that half chance.

'Good morning,' said Gutteridge to Browne, 'Do you mind telling me where you're from, and where you're both going?'

'Lea Bridge Road Garage; we've been out doing repairs,' was the reply. Gutteridge was not quite satisfied.

'Have you got a card?' he asked.

'No.'

'A driving licence?'

'No.'

'Where did you say you were from?' he asked again. Browne hesitated before repeating, 'The Lea Bridge Road garage.' By now Gutteridge was becoming suspicious. His next question, 'Is the car yours?' was answered by Kennedy,

'No, the car is mine.'

The policeman then shone his torch on the two men's faces before asking Kennedy if he knew the index number of the car. This time Browne replied, 'You will see it in front of the car.'

'I know the number,' Gutteridge replied, 'but do you?' Browne said, 'Yes, TW 6120.' Whether Gutteridge was still not entirely satisfied will never be known, but he put away his torch and took out his notebook and pencil saying, 'Very well, I will take particulars.'

Those were the last words he ever uttered, for they were immediately followed by two explosions. He staggered back mortally wounded and fell against the bank at the side of the road. Seconds later two more shots were fired, one through each of his eyes.

As dawn was breaking on Tuesday morning, the body of George Gutteridge was found by William Ward, a Post Office mail delivery contractor driving his van through How Green towards Abridge. After briefly examining the body, Ward ran along the road to tell a friend, Alfred Perritt, who lived a short distance away. While Perritt went into Havering-atte-Bower to inform PC Bloxham, the village constable, Ward continued into Stapleford Tawney from where he telephoned the police at Romford.

Events then moved swiftly. Soon after PC Bloxham arrived at the scene he was joined from Romford by Detective Inspector Crockford and Dr Robert Woodhouse. While Crockford made a careful examination of the scene, Dr Woodhouse carried out a brief examination of the body prior to performing a full post-mortem the next day. Crockford soon decided that the crime warranted the involvement of Scotland Yard with its expertise and facilities, to supplement the more limited resources of the local force.

Detective Chief Inspector William Berrett of Scotland Yard, deputed to take charge of the Gutteridge murder investigation, was a 'big' man in every sense of the word. Thick-set, with a neatly trimmed beard and moustache, Berrett usually wore a dark, heavy overcoat and a curly-brimmed, American-style trilby hat, tilted at a slightly rakish angle. He was to serve altogether just over thirty-eight years in the police force, and the Gutteridge case was to be the highlight of a successful CID career.

Upon receiving the call Berrett left at once for Essex accompanied by Detective Sergeant Harris, his assistant in many of the cases he investigated. At Romford they were apprised of the current situation before going to the murder scene, and then on to the coach house of the Royal Oak, where PC Gutteridge's body had been taken.

While discussing the case with local officers, Berrett was told of the last hour of Gutteridge's life. Of how he had left his home in Stapleford Abbots just before 3 a.m. on the Tuesday morning to make a pre-arranged meeting with PC Taylor from nearby Lambourne End. They rendezvoused just after 3 a.m., and for about twenty-five minutes the two men had chatted before parting, PC Taylor to continue his beat, Gutteridge to walk back in the direction of his home. It had been estimated that about ten minutes later, during which time he walked less than half-a-mile, Gutteridge met his death.

Berrett was particularly interested to learn that earlier on the Tuesday, a Dr Lovell from Billericay had reported that during the night his motor car, a blue Morris Cowley, had been stolen, and that two bullets had been recovered by Essex officers from the roadway beneath where PC Gutteridge had lain. These were to be of vital importance to the investigation.

The first major breakthrough came only hours later with the finding of the stolen motor car abandoned at the rear of a small house at Foxley Road, Brixton. Albert McDougall, a clerk, noticed the car when he left for work at 7.30 a.m. Finding it still there in the evening, he called at Brixton police station to notify them of its presence.

The vehicle was immediately driven to the police station where it had already been confirmed that it was the one that had been reported stolen earlier from Billericay. A thorough examination of the car by Detective Sergeant Hearne uncovered several vital clues, the most significant being an empty cartridge case bearing the mark RL 1V which he found near the front passenger seat. Hearne also found splashes of blood on the driver's running-board, and signs of recent damage to the front near-side mudguard indicating that the vehicle had come into contact with a grassy bank.

The same day a small tin cake box and a cardboard box, both containing ammunition, were found on waste ground in west London. When on the Wednesday a Mark V1 Webley service revolver was discovered on the Thames foreshore near Hammersmith Bridge the detectives' hopes were briefly raised, but it was soon established that none of these items were connected with the murder.

The day after PC Gutteridge's death, news of it appeared in the press alongside an account of another attack in which a pickpocket in London's City area tried to steal a watch from the pocket of eighty-year-old, veteran shipowner, Sir Walter Runciman. In the words of Sir Walter, 'I administered summary justice by a right upper-cut to the jaw, a useful blow I learned at sea ... he ran like blazes ...'

Sandwiched between that story and an announcement of the birth of a son to Signora Mussolini, wife of Italy's future dictator, was an item that illustrated that attitudes and responses may not have changed very much since the 1920s. At the National Provincial Union of Law Societies Conference in Sheffield, a man was bold enough to suggest when discussing the merits of women jurors that, 'Women were more emotional than men, and that their experience of commercial life, with some exceptions, was necessarily inferior to that of men.' This pronouncement drew from the secretary of a women's political organization the acid response that 'our critic has rather antediluvian ideas'. Later there were to be three women jurors at the trial of Browne and Kennedy.

In Romford on the Friday, the inquest into PC Gutteridge's death was opened. After hearing evidence of identification from his distraught widow, details of his last meeting with PC Taylor and the discovery of his body, the Coroner, Mr C.E. Lewis, adjourned the proceedings until 25 November.

The following day the funeral of PC Gutteridge took place at Christ Church, Warley, followed by interment at Warley cemetery. Apart from family, hundreds of mourners including a large contingent of policemen led by Captain Unett, the Chief Constable of Essex, heard the Bishop of Barking ask during his address, 'Did an Englishman do this?' a question echoed by many throughout the land.

Berrett needed no reminding that almost the entire population were anxious for him and his team to achieve success in their investigation. The majority of people were appalled at the cold-blooded ruthlessness displayed, and for that reason, if for no other, wanted the perpetrators caught. However, the desire of the less law-abiding fraternity to have them apprehended was inspired by a less altruistic motive, namely that of bringing to an end the intensive police activity which, devoted as it was to the capture of PC Gutteridge's killer(s), simultaneously curtailed their own activities.

By now his enquiries had convinced Berrett that he was seeking two people for the murder. Over the next weeks he and his team worked unceasingly in their hunt for the killers.

The exact, forty-three mile route taken by Browne and Kennedy, after leaving How Green until they abandoned their car in south London, was painstakingly retraced, entailing hours of house-to-house enquiries, and the questioning of hundreds of people. Dozens of letters and telephone calls were received at the murder headquarters offering help and information, and suggesting possible suspects. Most were intended to be helpful, although some were undoubtedly aimed at hindering the enquiry. All had to be diligently checked, and if necessary followed up – without the aid of modern day computers. The investigating officers travelled hundreds of miles in their quest, and scores of people were detained, questioned and then released, but the decisive breakthrough still eluded them.

Berrett had already shortlisted Frederick Guy Browne as a likely suspect. A check through Scotland Yard records had turned up his name early on as being among a select number of known criminals having the necessary attributes of ruthlessness, determination and hatred of the police essential in anyone prepared to commit such a cold-blooded killing. It was known also that Browne was familiar with the Essex countryside, so he fitted the bill perfectly.

If Berrett and his colleagues needed any extra incentive in the pursuit of their quarry, it was provided at the resumed inquest when Dr Woodhouse described his findings during the post-mortem he had carried out on the murdered constable.

'On the head there were two wounds in the left cheek ... surrounded by a scorched area about an eighth of an inch wide indicating that the muzzle of the weapon was held fairly close.' After describing the route taken by the bullets, and the injuries inflicted, the doctor continued, 'There were two other entry wounds, almost symmetrically placed, just below the eyeballs.' He explained that these would have caused death instantaneously and that the margin of the eye wounds were scorched and surrounded by an area of peppering caused by unburned granules of powder being forced into the skin, again indicating that the muzzle of the weapon when fired was less than six inches from the face. The doctor concluded that, 'four bullets had been fired into the head ... All four had been fired at close range and in my opinion those in the cheek were first received. The first was not serious, the second would have produced death by haemorrhage in two minutes, and the third and fourth would have caused instantaneous death. I would suggest that the last two shots were fired while the deceased lay on his back.'

After listening to Dr Woodhouse's harrowing testimony, Berrett had to admit reluctantly that he had 'not at present been able to trace the crime to the person or persons'. After briefly outlining the enquiries and progress so far made, he concluded unhappily, 'Unfortunately I have nothing definite, and enquiries are still being pursued.'

After the jury had predictably returned a verdict of 'wilful murder against some person or persons unknown', the Coroner, Mr Lewis, closed the proceedings with the words, 'Enquiries are proceeding in very good hands, and they [the jury] could rest assured that if there were any possibility of tracing the culprit no effort would be spared.'

After four months unceasing police activity, the hunt for Browne ended in January, 1928, with his arrest at his Battersea garage.

In November, 1927, a trivial motoring incident in Sheffield involving a Vauxhall motor car and another vehicle led to the discovery that the Vauxhall had been stolen from Tooting in south London. When later it was revealed that the Vauxhall had been sold to a local butcher for £100, and the trade-in of his

Angus-Sanderson, the Metropolitan detectives were notified. They already suspected Browne of being concerned in the theft, as his garage was not far from where the Vauxhall had been taken. Aware also that Detective Chief Inspector Berrett was anxious to question him regarding the Gutteridge murder, it was decided to mount a twenty-four hour watch on his garage.

The patience of the watching officers, led by Detective Inspector Barker and Detective Sergeant Miller, was rewarded when on the evening of Friday, 20 January, at about 8 p.m., a grey Angus-Sanderson, with Browne driving, turned into Northcote Road, Battersea, and then into the yard of the Globe Garage.

The arrest was carried out without incident; a posse of officers led by Detective Inspector Barker, after allowing sufficient time for him to enter, swiftly followed and surprised Browne, his wife and two mechanics who were questioned briefly and allowed to leave.

Barker turned to Browne and told him that he was to be arrested for stealing a Vauxhall motor car from Franciscan Road, Tooting, the previous November. Browne replied enigmatically, 'What do I know about stealing the car?' He said nothing more until whilst being searched a few minutes later a false driving licence in the name of Frederick Edwin Harris was found on him. When shown it he smilingly admitted that it was a 'dud' for use in case he was stopped. Other items found on him included surgical forceps, twelve cartridges and a mask. After these had been discovered, Browne remarked, 'There you are. You've got it now. That's the lot. You won't find anything else.'

No sooner had he said this than Detective Sergeant Bevis entered the office holding a .45 calibre Webley service revolver, no 351931, together with the six cartridges he had removed from the chamber. Bevis announced to Divisional Inspector Leach, 'I have just found this revolver fully loaded by the side of the driver's seat in the Angus-Sanderson car.' Before Leach could reply, Browne interrupted, 'Ah, you've found that have you? I'm done for now.' It was a prophetic remark; the gun recovered by Bevis was later proved to have been the murder weapon.

Things got even worse for Browne that Friday evening. A further search of his office revealed other medical items as would be found in a doctor's case. In the meantime Detective Sergeants Haines, Miller and Foley accompanied Mrs Browne to her home where yet more medical equipment was found, and where on top of a wardrobe Haines discovered a fully-loaded Smith and Wesson revolver in a leather case, together with thirty-four Mark IV cartridges. The next day searchers found another .45 Webley service revolver no 299431 hidden in a recess behind the driver's seat of the Angus-Sanderson.

Browne had been arrested for the theft of the Vauxhall, but the next morning he came face-to-face with Detective Chief Inspector Berrett, Divisional Inspector Leach, who had been present at his arrest, and Detective Sergeant Harris, all there to interview him in connection with the murder of PC Gutteridge.

Berrett introduced himself and the others to Browne, and told him that he was enquiring into the murder of PC Gutteridge. Without further preamble he then asked him if he could account for his movements on the night of 26 September 1927. Browne sat for some moments before replying; experienced as he was in police procedures, and aware of the risks attendant upon making a verbal or written statement, he was nonetheless conscious that on this occasion he was not being questioned in connection with a theft, burglary or even a robbery, but with a capital offence where an injudicious word or phrase could result in the hangman's rope being placed around his neck. Eventually he spoke, 'Why should I tell you anything? But there I might as well tell you about myself.'

It was a fateful decision. The two statements he dictated to Sergeant Harris on consecutive days were later proved to consist almost entirely of lies, evasions and denials. He denied having had knowledge of PC Gutteridge's murder until a policeman visiting his garage casually mentioned it. He told Sergeant Harris, 'I have no connection with the murder of PC Gutteridge, and I am not interested in it as it does not affect me.' He insisted that he had spent the night of 26/27 September at home with his wife, an alibi she later supported.

The various items found during the searches of his garage and home were laid out before him on the charge room table, and as he surveyed them, so he seemed to conceive spurious details of where he had obtained them, and reasons for having them.

The medical items he said he had bought at different chemists for use in case of an accident or emergency at his garage. The firearms and ammunition were more difficult to explain; he admitted having them in his possession, but with one important exception he refused to divulge their source. The exception was the murder weapon, Webley service revolver no 351931. This he said, he had bought for £3 from an unknown sailor at Tilbury the previous April. The ammunition for the weapon, which he insisted he had never fired, he said he had obtained from an ex-army friend.

Browne's insistence on having owned the Webley since the previous April was commented on at some length by Judge Avory during his summing-up. Browne told Sergeant Harris that he required the guns and ammunition as on two occasions when delivering cars he had been stopped and robbed. In future he wanted to be able to frighten off any would-be attackers.

He denied ever having driven through Essex at night, least of all having been party to the theft of a motor car.

He remained deliberately vague about the identity and whereabouts of Kennedy, no doubt suspecting that if caught his accomplice would not refrain from saying anything, or implicating anyone, in order to save his own skin. In the event the tracing and apprehension of Browne's partner was not long delayed. Word had reached Kennedy of Browne's arrest, and on Saturday morning while Browne was being interrogated at Tooting police station, he and his wife were on their way to Liverpool.

Berrett meantime learnt that a former acquaintance of Browne's in Sheffield may have information about his accomplice; he and Sergeant Harris therefore made the 350 mile round trip on the Monday in order to speak to him. Their journey was not in vain, as the informant came up with the name William Henry 'Pat' Kennedy.

Back in London enquiries at Kennedy's known haunts confirmed that he and his wife had departed hastily for Liverpool the day after Browne's arrest. Detective Inspector Kirschner and Detective Sergeant Duncan were the officers sent up to Merseyside with orders to liaise with local officers in finding and arresting Kennedy for being involved in the theft of the Vauxhall. The search lasted only two days, with the arrest being far more dramatic than had been that of Browne, almost resulting as it did in the shooting of another policeman.

The Kennedys were traced to a lodging-house at 119 Copperas Hill. On the late evening of 25 January, Inspector Kirschner and Sergeant Duncan, with Liverpool officers, were keeping observation on the address hoping Kennedy would appear. As it neared midnight a man emerged from the house and walked rapidly down Copperas Hill. It was Kennedy, and he was recognized by Detective Sergeant Mattinson, a local officer, who went after him.

As Mattinson approached the other man he said, 'Hello Bill, come on.' Kennedy's response was to produce an automatic pistol from his overcoat pocket, point it at the policeman and say, 'Stand back Bill, or I will shoot you.' Undeterred Mattinson closed with the other man and a short scuffle ensued during the course of which Kennedy squeezed the trigger of his pistol which mercifully still had the safety-catch on. Mattinson then overpowered Kennedy and handed him to Kirschner and Duncan who by this time had caught up.

At the police station Kennedy's revolver was found to have a round in the barrel and seven more in the magazine. When his lodgings were searched a second, fully-loaded magazine was found.

Kennedy, accompanied by his wife, was escorted back to London, and on the following morning he in turn was confronted at Scotland Yard by Detective Chief Inspector Berrett. Berrett told him that he was to be charged with stealing the Vauxhall motor car, and followed up by saying to him, 'I have been making enquiries for some time past respecting the murder of PC Gutteridge. Can you give me any information about that occurrence?' Kennedy replied,

'I may be able to tell you something. Let me consider.' He sat for some moments, head in his hands, deep in thought. Finally he asked, 'Can I see my wife?' This was agreed to and Mrs Kennedy was called into the room.

For her, married only a few weeks, the past four days had been a nightmare. The hasty departure for Liverpool from their south London home; her husband's jumpiness since their arrival, his dash from the house and his arrest the previous night, and now this room where he sat surrounded by grim-faced policemen.

'You know, my dear,' her husband began, 'that when I was arrested at Liverpool yesterday I told you I thought it was something more serious than stealing a car. These officers are enquiring about that policeman murdered in Essex.'

The nightmare was continuing.

'You didn't murder him did you?'

'No I didn't,' her husband replied, 'but I was there and I know who did.' Those nine words condemned Kennedy to the gallows.

He continued, 'If I am charged with murder and found guilty I shall be hanged and you will be a widow. On the other hand if I am charged and found guilty of being an accessory after the fact I shall

receive a long sentence of penal servitude and I shall be a long time
away from you. Will you wait for me?'
    'Yes love, I will wait for you anytime.'
    'What shall I do then?'
    'Tell these gentlemen the truth of what took place.'
    'All right, I will.'
    If Browne had been present when Kennedy made his statement
to Sergeant Harris, his doubts about his accomplice would have
been confirmed.
    The statement commenced ingenuously enough with Kennedy
describing his employment at Browne's garage. Moving on to
events that took place on the night of the murder, he said that it
was at Browne's suggestion that they had gone to Billericay to steal
a car. He described the theft of the Morris Cowley, and their drive
through the lanes and minor roads of Essex until they were
signalled to stop. Kennedy recounted the conversation they had
both had with PC Gutteridge culminating in Browne shooting the
policeman. He went on, 'I saw the policeman stagger back, and he
fell back to the hedge against the bank. I said to Browne, "What
have you done?" and I saw he had a revolver in his hand. He said,
"Get out quick." I got out. The policeman was on his back.
Browne said, "I will finish the bastard." I said, "For God's sake
don't shoot anymore. The man is dying." His eyes were open and
he was groaning.'
    He told how Browne had shot Gutteridge through the eyes and
continued, 'Browne then said, "Let us get back into the car." We
had driven close into the bank and now backed out and drove in
the direction of Ongar. He gave me a revolver and told me to load it
but in my excitement I dropped an empty shell in the car. ...'
Kennedy then said that Browne had asked him if he had loaded the
gun, and if so to give it to him. 'I gave it to him and he kept it on
the seat at his side.'
    Kennedy told of how they had returned to London and
abandoned the car, and how unbeknown to him, Browne had kept
some of Dr Lovell's instruments. It seems that Kennedy had been
worried after their return to London, as he said he had suggested to
Browne that they move away. Browne's response to this idea was
uncompromising. 'Browne said there was no danger and said if I
made up my mind to leave him, he would blow my brains out. He
had a pistol in his hand at the time, and I believed him.'
    Nonetheless Kennedy did leave London briefly to journey up to

West Kirby, where he got married. On 14 January he returned to London with his wife and took a furnished flat previously occupied by the Brownes at 2 Huguenot Place, Wandsworth, where they remained until they fled to Liverpool eight days later.

Kennedy ended his statement by saying that he had seen Browne with two loaded Webleys and plenty of ammunition, and that Browne had told him that he also possessed a Smith and Wesson and another small revolver. It is hardly surprising that Browne exploded with fury in court when first he heard his erstwhile friend's statement.

The first time that Browne and Kennedy stood in the dock together was on the following Monday, when they appeared at the South-Western police court charged jointly with the theft of the Vauxhall motor car from Tooting. Detective Chief Inspector Berrett told the magistrate, Mr Sandbach, when applying for a week's remand, that another charge against them both was pending.

So it was that a week later on Monday 6 February 1928, at half-past-eight in the morning, Berrett saw the two men at Lavender Hill police station and charged them with Gutteridge's murder. Kennedy remained silent, while Browne replied, 'You are charging me with murder. It is absurd. I know nothing about it.' Two hours later they were again before Mr Sandbach at the start of the lengthy proceedings that were to end eight weeks later with their committal for trial to the Old Bailey.

The police court hearings and subsequent trial of Browne and Kennedy for the murder of PC Gutteridge attracted enormous, countrywide interest. In the United States the prohibition era had seen countless gangland killings as hoodlum chiefs jealously protected their territory and illegal business interests, but at home the trial of two men for the murder of a village 'bobby' was of far greater interest, as the columns of space devoted in the newspapers to reporting the proceedings indicated. At each of the police court hearings, and later at the Old Bailey, swarms of people jostled each other in an attempt to get into court. Most were unlucky, and they lined the pavements for a hundred yards on either side of the court entrances, hoping for a glimpse of the accused men as they arrived or departed.

In court both men seemed aware that they were the centre of attention. With one exception they remained composed throughout, occasionally smiling to their wives, or leaning over the dock rail to have a whispered consultation with their legal advisors.

Each was well dressed, Kennedy taking particular care over his appearance. On one occasion he stood in the dock resplendent in a new brown suit with a mauve collar, a speckled tie and sporting tortoise-shell rimmed pince-nez. Their wives equally vied with each other in their stylishness, although Mrs Kennedy's appearance at one hearing wearing a brick-red coat with a posy of geraniums on the collar, may have struck onlookers as being less appropriate in the circumstances than the fur-trimmed black coat worn by Mrs Browne.

In the dock with a uniformed policeman separating them, and two plain-clothes officers behind, their husbands listened as the prosecution witnesses were introduced by Mr H.D. Roome, the Crown counsel. Early in the proceedings it became apparent that the police had assembled a formidable case. From the moment during the prosecutor's opening address, when he mentioned the three bullets found at the scene, and their matching the gun that had fired them, to the final day of the hearing when a succession of firearms experts gave evidence, the defence must have been well aware of the immense task that lay ahead if Browne and Kennedy were to walk out of court as free men.

Several dramatic moments enlivened proceedings during their nine appearances at the police court: Mrs Gutteridge's weeping, as, watched by the accused and their wives, she told the court of the last time she had seen her husband alive, and of how later she had identified his mutilated body. The reading of Browne and Kennedy's statements, the former completely denying knowledge of, or involvement in, the murder, Kennedy denying involvement, if not knowledge. Immediately after Kennedy's statement had been read, Browne leapt to his feet and shouted at Mr Sandbach, the magistrate, 'I hope you are all well-satisfied. It has been well put together and concocted by the police.' Mr Sandbach told him to be quiet, whereupon Browne sank back on to his chair, muttering audibly, 'I hope you are satisfied.'

More drama followed. There was the suggestion put to Detective Chief Inspector Berrett that Kennedy's statement had been taken under duress, and when he was exhausted after his train journey from Liverpool. This proposition was vigorously denied by the policeman.

The moment when, as evidence of the finding of the bullets at the scene was being given, Browne produced a copy of the *Christian Herald* newspaper upon which to rest the notepaper on which he was writing.

Dr Lovell's evidence as to the theft, recovery and subsequent identification of his car, and his testifying that the case and instruments found in Browne's possession were 'similar' to those he had left in his vehicle.

The telegram bearing the fake message, 'Come at once. Sister seriously ill. Stay indefinitely. Kitty', sent by Kennedy to himself at 2 Huguenot Place, which he used as an excuse for him and his wife to leave hurriedly on 21 January for Liverpool.

Finally, Mrs Kennedy's loud protest in court on 6 March, that a man had been sketching her. Mr Sandbach assured her that enquiries would be made into the allegation.

At last the prosecution finished, their witnesses all heard and their testimony recorded. Mr O'Connor and Mr Tomkins on behalf of Browne and Kennedy, told the court that both men would plead not guilty and reserve their defence, following which Mr Sandbach committed them both for trial at the Central Criminal Court.

The trial of Browne and Kennedy opened at the Old Bailey on Monday, 23 April 1928, before Mr Justice Avory. Prosecuting for the Crown was the recently appointed Solicitor-General, Sir F. Boyd Merriman, KC, assisted by Mr H.D. Roome and Miss Enid Rosser, who had the unique distinction of being the first female barrister to participate in an Old Bailey trial.

Mr E.F. Lever for Browne, and Mr F.J. Powell for Kennedy, both made immediate application for their clients to be tried separately, on the grounds that their respective answers to the charge were incompatible with each other. Despite their pleas, it was Sir Boyd Merriman's argument that the two accused were jointly concerned in an illegal enterprise that had ended in murder that prevailed, with Mr Justice Avory dismissing the applications with the observation that 'no reasonable ground has been shown for making an order for separate trials'.

Although a queue for admittance had formed three hours earlier, only a limited number of spectators were admitted into court, the rest prevented from entering by a barrier placed across the entrance.

When the trial got underway the first day was mainly taken up by Sir Boyd Merriman's opening address, in which he described the circumstances of the crime, the investigation that followed and the arrest of the accused men. Kennedy was dismayed to hear the Solicitor-General shatter the hope he had of transferring blame for the murder on to Browne by saying, 'Let me say at once that the statement is against Kennedy alone. It is not to be taken as evidence against Browne ... The case for the Crown is that Police Constable Gutteridge was shot by one or both of these men.'

The trial's second day was largely devoted to evidence of Browne's arrest, the searching of his garage and home and the discovery of the various weapons, ammunition and doctor's equipment. Later, Dr Roche Lynch, the senior official Home Office analyst, went into the witness box and pointed out several spots that he had identified as human blood stains on a motor car running board.

Dr Lovell of Billericay testified to the loss, finding and examination of his motor car, stating that it was undamaged when he had driven it into his garage. He was shown a doctor's case and a number of surgical instruments, all of which he said belonged to him. It was later rumoured that Dr Lovell never reclaimed his motor car from the police, preferring instead to spend £142.10.0 (£142.50) on a new 11.9 hp 2-door Morris Cowley.

The trial took a dramatic turn when Detective Sergeant Mattinson gave evidence of Kennedy's arrest. The court was hushed as Sergeant Mattinson described how the 'prisoner suddenly switched round facing me, at the same time drawing his hand out of the right-hand pocket of his overcoat, and thrust the muzzle of a pistol between the point of my ribs. I heard a distinct click'. When Mr Powell, Kennedy's counsel suggested that, 'Is it not a gross exaggeration to say that he tried to shoot you?' Mattinson replied, 'I believe that he did.'

The day ended with Detective Chief Inspector Berrett detailing the circumstances in which the written statements were obtained from the two accused.

Wednesday, the halfway stage in the trial, was taken up at the beginning with the evidence of ballistics experts. George Henry Ibbetson, late lieutenant in the Royal Artillery, now an Assistant Inspector of small-arms ammunition at the Royal Arsenal, Woolwich, had examined all the ammunition produced in the case, and of that found in Browne's pocket he said that all the .45 calibre could be fired from a Webley revolver.

The most impressive of the Crown's firearms experts was Mr

Robert Churchill, a West End gunsmith with a lifetime's experience of small-arms. He had been handed the various weapons and ammunition found by police for comparison. After giving a wealth of technical detail relating to the type of cartridge used and whether they were cordite or black powder filled, he was asked by Sir Boyd Merriman about the cartridge case found in Dr Lovell's car. 'Did you form an opinion as to whether the cartridge case was fired from some Webley revolver in particular?' Churchill replied that he had examined both the Webleys found in the Angus-Sanderson. 'From microscopical examination it is possible for me to say that the empty cartridge case found in Dr Lovell's car was fired from the revolver found in the pocket near the driver's seat in Browne's car and from no other.'

Two other experts, William Henry Fox, Chief Examiner at the small-arms factory at Enfield Lock, and George Henry Perry, a chemist at the Royal Arsenal, Woolwich, had both reached the same conclusions as Churchill. The unanimity of the firearms experts as to the weapon that had fired the fatal shots virtually condemned Browne, if not Kennedy, to the gallows.

Churchill had also examined the .38 calibre revolver used by Kennedy in his attempt to shoot Sergeant Mattinson.

'Have you tested the safety catch?' he was asked by Sir Boyd Merriman.

'Yes, and it is rather hard to operate,' he answered.

'Did you try the pistol by firing eight shots from it?' was the next question.

'Yes, it was in perfect working order,' the expert replied. Those two answers showed just how close Sergeant Mattinson had been to sharing Gutteridge's fate.

Before the defence case opened there had been speculation that the underlying resentment that simmered between Browne and Kennedy might erupt into open hostility when the time came for them each to give his answer to the charge. To many people's surprise their attitude towards each other continued to be restrained.

Mr Lever spoke first. He emphasized that from the time of his arrest Browne had steadfastly maintained his innocence. Browne's wife, said Mr Lever, would later state under oath that she and her husband had spent the night of the murder together in bed.

When Browne went into the witness box he did little to further his case, or endear himself to the jury. At the outset, when required to take the oath, he told Mr Justice Avory, 'I cannot take this oath. How can I swear to the whole truth? I shall never know the whole truth about this thing.' In the end he reluctantly complied after being told by the judge that he had no alternative except to make an unsworn statement from the dock. It was an unpropitious start. His arrogance turned spectators in court instinctively against him, but he still persisted in his denials, convinced of his ability to persuade his audience.

When Kennedy's statement was referred to, he scornfully dismissed it saying, 'It is a carefully concocted statement that has taken hours to consider in my opinion.' When asked again later by Mr Lever if there was any truth in Kennedy's statement, Browne repeated, 'It is a fairy tale from beginning to end. I do not know how he started it or brought it about. But I can give a very good reason why.'

'Have you ever threatened to shoot Kennedy?'

'I have never threatened him in any way except to tell him that he must not persist in getting drunk and making a beast of himself.'

'Have you ever fired a single shot from this revolver?'

'I have never fired a shot.'

Browne went on to contest that the items of medical equipment identified by Dr Lovell did in fact belong to the doctor. He tried to explain that they were the tools of his trade, but again his condescension irritated his listeners. 'I'm not just a mechanic you know. That's what you people don't understand. I'm a motor engineer and my instruments are far different to your average garage man. I do better class work ... That's why I use surgical forceps as pliers ... The police are talking a load of rubbish, twisting things round. That thing they say is an ear speculum. That is for testing sparking plugs. You never see a doctor driving round with such an instrument. I know that if they don't.'

Finally, when referring to his arrest, Browne raised an unintentional laugh when he said, 'They [the police], intimated that they would have blown me to bits if I had made any resistance. But they were in quite a good temper about it and were laughing.'

Mr Powell, Kennedy's counsel, stood up. 'Did you not pull that revolver out on the spur of the moment after Kennedy had asked you to stop the car to see what the Constable wanted?'

'I am not in the habit of pulling revolvers out on the spur of the moment.'

Mr Powell paused: 'After shooting him [Gutteridge], were you not in a state of frenzy, and did not Kennedy ask you not to shoot again?'

'You are building on a rotten foundation – a foundation of lies.'

'Didn't Kennedy say, "Don't shoot any more, the man's dying"?'

'That is imagination on the part of a drunkard.'

'And then you shot Gutteridge in both eyes?'

'I have never fired a revolver in my life.'

Browne's testimony ended as it had started, by his again crossing swords with Mr Justice Avory. Before leaving the witness box he complained that his evidence had been twisted round. The judge replied severely, 'Don't talk to me about twisting things around. I am reading the evidence which you gave.' As Browne continued to argue, Mr Justice Avory told him, 'I am not going to bandy words with you about the evidence.' The court was silent as Browne returned to the dock after almost three hours in the witness box.

On Thursday Kennedy elected to make his statement less credibly from the dock unsworn, thereby avoiding the ordeal of cross-examination.

Kennedy's attitude was as unctuous as had Browne's been arrogant. Leaning casually on the dock rail he looked at the jury and addressed them conversationally. 'Ladies and gentlemen,' he began, 'the statement I made to Inspector Berrett is absolutely true … I had not the slightest idea on the night of the murder that Browne was carrying a revolver.' He went on to tell the jury that after the shooting, 'I was absolutely terrified by the way he acted. The man was in absolutely a mad frenzy. It was that which caused me to reload the revolver … I did not really know what I was doing.'

The pistol that he had been carrying at the time of his arrest he said had been given to him by Browne. He had been frightened that had he given information to the police, they would have been immediately aware of his presence at the murder scene, and would have accused him, 'although I was completely innocent of it'. He left his most sycophantic utterance to the end when he virtuously said, 'I can only now express my deep regret to Mrs Gutteridge that I should have been in the car on the night of the murder.'

It is hardly surprising that Mr Lever, when making his closing speech on behalf of Browne, should have launched into a scathing attack against Kennedy and his statement. 'When Kennedy made that statement nothing was sacred to him except his safety – the one thought of the caged rat.' In fact, no one was more aware than Mr Lever of how damaging Kennedy's statement was to his client's case. He continued discrediting Kennedy by reminding the jury that he had opted out of giving evidence on oath and submitting himself to cross-examination. Instead he had 'taken all the advantage of a coward's screen by the panel of the dock'. The irresistible inference, Browne's counsel suggested, was that the fatal shots were fired from Kennedy's revolver and not from Browne's.

Returning again to Kennedy's statement, Mr Lever said, 'The statement is a sort of historical novel, in which you get some true facts worked in with fiction to suit the requirements of the writer.' He ended his peroration to the jury by urging them that, 'All the efforts of the prosecution had failed to produce the slightest evidence that Browne was anywhere near the scene of the murder on the night of 26 September.'

When Mr Powell rose to make his final speech on Kennedy's behalf, the spectators were enthralled at the verbal duel taking place between counsel for the accused men.

Mr Powell launched straight into the attack by asserting that the evidence that had been given in court during the preceding three days, including Kennedy's statement which he said had been corroborated by many of the prosecution witnesses, pointed irrefutably to his innocence, and that there had therefore been no need for Kennedy to enter the witness box and submit himself to needless cross-examination. In Mr Powell's submission, Kennedy had not been aware that Browne was in possession of a gun until the first two shots were fired. On that premise it followed that Kennedy could not have been a party to the shooting.

Mr Powell did his best to project Kennedy in a better light than he himself had succeeded in doing. After pointing out that in his statement Kennedy had said that he had begged Browne not to fire again, Mr Powell asked, 'Does that show the monster and callous brute? Does it not show that although he may be a burglar, he is not a murderer.' Before ending, Mr Powell made reference again to Kennedy's arrest, repeating his view that Detective Sergeant Mattinson had exaggerated the events that had taken place. Kennedy, he insisted, had done nothing worse than try to bluff the officer.

Before Mr Justice Avory summed-up, Sir Boyd Merriman

addressed the court. He made it clear that there was no suggestion that the two accused went out on the night of 26 September 1927 with the intention of shooting a policeman, but rather that if one was unfortunate enough to interfere with their illegal activities, they were quite prepared to shoot their way out. Such had been PC Gutteridge's terrible misfortune that night.

He expressed his amazement that Browne and Kennedy had not disposed of the incriminating doctor's instruments, and went on to say that in his view it was absurd to suggest that Browne did not have the murder weapon in his possession at the time of the murder. The Solicitor-General suggested to the court that Kennedy also had a revolver on the fatal night.

Sir Boyd Merriman agreed that Kennedy's statement was completely accurate on matters that could be challenged, no doubt in the hope he said, that this would give added credence to the vitally important, if less factual parts of the statement it was essential for him to have believed.

Judge Horace Avory was seventy-seven years old when he presided at the trial of Browne and Kennedy in 1928. Acclaimed as the country's finest criminal judge, with his pursed lips, blinking eyes and quiet, precise manner, he was often the butt of carefully disguised humour among his colleagues.

Frederick Browne and William Kennedy were soon aware that appearance notwithstanding, they were facing a judge who seemingly had missed not a single point that had been made both for and against them during the preceding four days.

Mr Justice Avory told the jury that there were four points for them to consider:

1   Was PC Gutteridge murdered on 26 September 1927?
2   Was the murder committed by the person or persons who had stolen Dr Lovell's motor car?
3   Were the two prisoners in the doctor's car at the time the murder was committed?
4   If so, who shot the police constable? If only one of them did so, were they working in concert to prevent their detention or arrest?

When referring to Browne, and the first Webley revolver found in the Angus-Sanderson, Mr Justice Avory asked, 'Was Browne in possession of that revolver on the night of 26

September? ... Browne said, "I have never fired the revolver since
I first had it. I got it sometime in April last ... " Could they doubt
that the revolver from which the cartridge had been fired – the
empty cartridge found in the car – had been in his possession since
the previous April? In the witness box he admitted in the plainest
possible terms that this was the revolver to which he was
referring ...'

Moving on to Kennedy's alleged involvement, the judge said
that, 'If the jury came to the conclusion that Browne was in the car
and fired the shot – or any of the shots – they must ask themselves
whether Kennedy was aiding and abetting Browne in the killing of
PC Gutteridge in order to prevent their arrest.' After explaining
briefly the law regarding 'aiding and abetting', Mr Justice Avory
continued, 'If Kennedy at the time the police constable was shot,
knew that he was being shot in the execution of his duty, and if the
jury were of the opinion that Kennedy was acting in consort with
Browne in shooting that constable in order to prevent their arrest
or further detention, then he was liable to be found guilty on this
indictment.'

Horace Avory concluded by telling the jury, 'If you are satisfied
beyond any reasonable doubt that both these prisoners were guilty
of shooting the police constable, you will fearlessly and without
hesitation say so, and if you can see a reason to distinguish
between them you will equally fearlessly and without hesitation
say so.'


'In both cases we find the prisoner guilty.' As the jury foreman
spoke the fateful words, the silence of the court was punctuated by
a sudden outburst of sobbing from Mrs Kennedy. Her husband
and Browne remained unflinching; the extra prison warders who
had been drafted in to prevent a possible attack by Browne on his
accomplice, relaxed.

Before sentence was passed both men addressed the court.

'Your Lordship,' said Browne, 'The Court, according to law,
has found me guilty of wilful murder. I cannot alter what the
court has done, I do not desire to. I will admit here and now
that the counsel have acted very fairly as far as I am
concerned. I admit that I would not wish to be tried by a

better judge, but the jury have had stuff given to them which is not genuine. It is the fault of the way in which it has been put together. I can only say that it will come out later on that I had nothing to do with it, but I am not going to argue the point. I am not going to try to prove my case, and the simple reason is that there is something hanging over my head so that, if I got off all this, I should get penal servitude for something else, which is far worse than this is for me. I am quite content to leave it that I am not guilty according to the One above, who can know; but the court says that I am. I am quite content. My conscience is clear.'

Kennedy, although briefer, tended to intellectualize:

'Nothing I can say now will alter the verdict. It was pre-ordained. It was fate, and you, however fairly you have tried the case, and the jury, are mere instruments of that fate. I speak in no mere spirit of bravado when I say that I am not afraid of death, but that I am dying willingly because I have the certain knowledge that in the hereafter I shall be united in all eternity to the one darling girl who has stuck to me through all this ordeal.'

He then thanked his counsel and asked if he might be allowed to speak to his wife.

Judge Avory reminded them that they had been found guilty of a 'most foul and brutal murder', before he donned the black cap and sentenced them to death. As with the verdict, both men remained unmoved, and for the last time Browne smiled at his wife as he stepped out of sight from the dock.

Three weeks later the appeals of Browne and Kennedy were heard. Counsel for both of them submitted that their being tried together had resulted in a miscarriage of justice, and that the trial judge had misdirected the jury.

Only Kennedy was present to hear Lord Hewart, the Lord Chief Justice, review at length both the circumstances of the case and the grounds of appeal, before announcing that he and his fellow Judges of Appeal, Mr Justice Salter and Mr Justice Branson, could find no grounds for interfering with either the verdict or sentence.

With the dismissal of their appeals went the last realistic hope either man may have had of escaping the gallows. There was to be no last minute reprieve. At nine o'clock precisely on the morning of Thursday, 31 May 1928, Frederick Guy Browne was executed at Pentonville, while across London his accomplice, William Henry Kennedy, suffered the same fate at Wandsworth.

Mrs Browne was absent from the crowd outside Pentonville, but Mrs Kennedy, after first attending Mass, arrived by taxi at the prison gates shortly before the execution was due to take place. She was weeping bitterly and in a state of collapse as the prison clock struck nine. Unfortunately she was then recognized by the crowd, many of whom swarmed round her cab to witness her grief, before police cleared a path for the taxi to leave.

On the eve of his execution Kennedy had written a last message to his wife,

'Time is getting short, sweetheart, and still I feel that strange calm and confidence of our reunion. Perhaps the worst is to know the exact hour, and yet perhaps the best. Darling my last word. I again assert that I had no previous knowledge of what was going to happen that night. I go to my death knowing that, and that my statement was true, and that my own darling believes me.'

There is no record of Browne having similarly written to his wife, although she sent him a final telegram of farewell.

Aside from the murder itself, which was committed with a rare callousness, the Gutteridge case is remembered for two notable features; the coming of age of the science of ballistics, and the degree of teamwork and co-operation that existed between Scotland Yard and a provincial force.

Like all new sciences, ballistics was regarded with scepticism prior to the Gutteridge trial. There the testimony of Robert Churchill and the other experts convinced the doubters that an impressive new aid in the battle against the armed criminal had arrived. Goddard's Comparison Microscope enabled cartridge cases to be compared. In the Gutteridge case the marks imprinted on the cartridge case found in the Morris Cowley matched exactly the marks on a test cartridge fired from the Webley service revolver No 351931 found in the driver's door pocket of the Angus-Sanderson, thus proving beyond doubt that that was the murder weapon. If Kennedy in his nervousness had not carelessly dropped the used cartridge case on to the floor of the motor car, the case against Browne would have been infinitely more difficult to prove.

The co-operation between the Metropolitan and Essex officers investigating the case was a welcome change from the petty jealousies that hitherto had often been apparent among provincial police forces when Scotland Yard was called in on a major investigation. Sadly this resentment continued to simmer among some forces for years after the Gutteridge case. Nowadays with the introduction of Regional Crime Squads, and with most police forces having superb forensic and other resources of their own, the divide that formerly existed has all but been eliminated.

Thus it was that a combination of scientific expertise in a new field and force co-operation together helped solve a crime that had aroused the horror of the nation during the inter-war years.

*Postscript:*

Following a report from Captain Unett in which he praised the efforts of Detective Chief Inspector Berrett and Detective Sergeant Harris during the Gutteridge inquiry, the Administration Sub-Committee of the Essex Standing Joint Committee, sitting at Chelmsford on Wednesday, 6 June 1928, announced that they 'had informed the Commissioner of Police that they would be pleased to hear that the above-mentioned officers [Berrett and Harris], will receive some reward for the meritorious manner in which they conducted the enquiries'.

I can find no record as to whether such a reward was ever made.

# Bibliography

Benson, L., *The Book of Remarkable Trials and Notorious Characters* (John Camden Hotten, 1872)

Berrett, James, *When I was at Scotland Yard* (Sampson Low, Marsten)

Cherrill, Fred, *Cherrill of the Yard* (Geo. G. Harrap, 1954)

Graham, Evelyn, *Fifty Years of Famous Judges* (John Long)

Hall, John, *The Trial of Herbert John Bennett* (Geoffrey Bles, 1929)

Henderson, William, ed., *Trial of William Gardiner* (Butterworth, 1934)

Honeycombe, Gordon, *The Murders of the Black Museum 1870-1970* (Hutchinson, 1982)

Jesse, F. Tennyson, ed., *Trial of Samuel Herbert Dougal* (William Hodge, 1928)

Packer, Edwin, *The Peasenhall Murder* (Yoxford Publications, 1980)

Phillips, Janet and Peter, *Victorians at Home and Away* (Croom Helm, 1978)

Savage, Percy, *Savage of Scotland Yard* (Hutchinson)

Shore, W. Teignmouth, ed., *Trial of James Blomfield Rush* (William Hodge, 1928)

Simpson, Keith, *Forty Years of Murder* (Geo. G. Harrap, 1978)

Totterdell, G.H., *Country Copper* (Geo. G. Harrap, 1956)

Wilson, Colin, and Pitman, Patricia, *Encyclopaedia of Murder* (Arthur Barker, 1961)

The files of *The Times, Daily Mirror, Eastern Daily Press, Eastern Evening News, Brentwood Gazette, Southend Standard Recorder, Essex Times, Norfolk Chronicle* and *Norwich Gazette, Norfolk Press, Illustrated London News, Cambridge News, The Sunday Telegraph Magazine.*